Computers and Local Government

Kenneth L. Kraemer
John Leslie King

The Praeger Special Studies program—utilizing the most modern and efficient book production techniques and a selective worldwide distribution network—makes available to the academic, government, and business communities significant, timely research in U.S. and international economic, social, and political development.

Computers and Local Government

Volume 1, A Manager's Guide

PRAEGER SPECIAL STUDIES IN U.S. ECONOMIC, SOCIAL, AND POLITICAL ISSUES

83359

Praeger Publishers   New York   London

Library of Congress Cataloging in Publication Data

Kraemer, Kenneth L
    Computers and local government.

    (Praeger special studies in U.S. economic, social,
and political issues)
    Vol. 2 edited by K. L. Kraemer and J. L. King.
    Bibliography: p.
    CONTENTS: v. 1. A manager's guide. —v. 2. A
review of research.
    1. Local government—United States—Data processing.
I. King, John Leslie, joint author. II. Title.
JS344.E4K68   1977   352'.00028'54   77-23886

This book was prepared with the support of the National Science Founda-
tion, Research Applied to National Needs Division, under grant numbers
GI-39068 and APR74-12158-A01. The views expressed herein are those of the
authors, and should not be ascribed as the views of the National Science
Foundation. Reproduction in whole or part permitted for any purpose of the
United States Government.

PRAEGER SPECIAL STUDIES
200 Park Avenue, New York, N.Y., 10017, U.S.A.

Published in the United States of America in 1977
by Praeger Publishers,
A Division of Holt, Rinehart and Winston, CBS, Inc.

789 038 987654321

Printed in the United States of America

This book is dedicated to
Norine Kraemer and Kathleen King,
whose patience and support have sustained us.

Public Policy Research Organization and
Graduate School of Administration
University of California, Irvine

PROLOGUE

Computer technology offers one of the major hopes for increasing the productivity and effectiveness of local governments. Proper use of computers can improve operations by providing better managerial control of programs and departments and bring about improved planning and decisionmaking through new capabilities for data analysis. Proper use may even reduce costs of certain activities. The hope that computers will assist local governments is evidenced by the large number of cities and counties that now use computers.

The key to realizing the benefits of computers is proper management and use. For the past fifteen years, the International City Management Association, the National League of Cities, and the National Association of Counties have actively promoted improved use of computers through training programs, conferences, and publications. We believe that these efforts have resulted in better utilization of computers by local governments and in the expansion of functions to which computers have been applied.

From time to time it is necessary to take stock of the progress that has been made and the lessons that have been learned in order to guide further planning and development efforts. *Computers and Local Government* presents the findings of the first large-scale evaluation of research literature on computers in local government. This book presents policy advice and recommendations based on the most current and reliable information available on the subject. It is organized in a clear and direct format that will allow government managers and their staff members to easily use it. It is a comprehensive, well written, and sensible contribution to a subject that deserves the careful attention of every local government. We recommend this book to all who are interested in improving local government use of computers.

Alan Beals, Executive Director
National League of Cities

Bernie Hillenbrand, Executive Director
National Association of Counties

Mark Keane, Executive Director
International City Management
Association

PREFACE

This two-volume book summarizes the findings and conclusions of a study called "Evaluation of Policy-Related Research in Municipal Information Systems" (EPRIS for short). This project was carried out in 1974 and 1975 by the Urban Information Systems Research Group (URBIS) of the Public Policy Research Organization (PPRO) at the University of California, Irvine, and supported by a grant from the National Science Foundation. The purpose of the EPRIS Project was to collect and study all the available research and professional literature on information systems that might relate to local governments. The findings and conclusions from this study, as presented in this book, are addressed to two audiences: managers, practitioners and professionals in government who work with or have an interest in computers and data processing; and students and researchers interested in information technology and public management.

These two volumes present material arranged according to five topic areas: planning and management, financial considerations, personnel and manpower policy, computer technology, and privacy and disclosure issues. The first volume presents policy-related conclusions from the EPRIS Project specifically for managers and policymakers who deal with computers. It refers for support to sections of the second volume, but does not reference original source materials. The second volume presents actual research findings relevant to computers in local government, and references original works reviewed in the project. An extensive bibliography is provided in the second volume. A reading of both volumes will provide a thorough introduction to research knowledge in this field.

For those who wish to go beyond the findings and conclusions presented in these volumes, the original research reports from the EPRIS Project are available from the National Technical Information Service (NTIS). These reports are listed in the Bibliography to this volume with their NTIS catalogue numbers. Also, for those with an interest in the role of the local government executive in information systems, a monograph entitled *Computers, Power, and Urban Management: What Every Local Executive Should Know* is available from Sage Publications. This report is also listed in the Bibliography.

As the PPRO list in the Bibliography suggests, the initial output of the EPRIS project was voluminous. Furthermore, each of the ten reports was written as a stand-alone document with its own managers' guide, policy recommendations, methodology, research synthesis, research reviews and bibliography. As we sent out the final reports for review by practitioners and academics, it became apparent that the quantity of material was too great to disseminate effectively to all of the intended audiences. Therefore, we undertook the task of preparing this book.

Volume 1, *A Manager's Guide*, is based in large part upon the ten research reports, but is essentially an original construction containing material which goes beyond or was omitted in the project reports. Volume 2, *A Review of the Research* is based upon the substantive portions of the project reports, but has been considerably condensed and rewritten with the subsequent approval of the original authors.

We would like to acknowledge the contributions of others to this work. Most important is the work of the other members of the EPRIS research staff: George Duggar, Robert Emrey, Linda Hackathorn, Richard Hackathorn, Henry Lucas, Joseph Matthews, Frances Mossman, and AnnaBelle Sartore. These colleagues share in the credit for these two volumes, and it is fair to say that they are all co-authors. Four other members of the URBIS Research Group, James Danziger, William H. Dutton, Rob Kling, and Alana Northrop, all made room in their busy research schedules to review and comment on these volumes. Our research assistants, Mark Burnett, Doug Cline, James Lyons, and Erin Miller provided intelligent and enthusiastic assistance throughout the project.

We would also like to express our deep appreciation to the following local government practitioners and experts who contributed their comments and criticism to this work: Myron Weiner of the Institute of Public Service at the University of Connecticut; Taguchi Tamaru, Director of Data Services of the City of Los Angeles; Donald Luria, President of the Urban and Regional Information Systems Association (URISA); Ralph Young, Director of Computer Systems Development for Fairfax County, Virginia; Owen Griffith and Matt King, Technology Advisors of the California Innovation Group; Tom Bruderlee of the National Association of Counties; Phil Wynn of Public Technology, Incorporated; and Matt McDonald, Executive Director of the State of California Intergovernmental Board on Electronic Data Processing.

The PPRO Professional Staff rendered essential support throughout the project, and deserve special mention for their patience and competence. David Schetter, Sheila Grattan, Doris McBride, and Shirley Hoberman helped keep the wheels of progress moving, and were of great help to Joseph Matthews who performed the duties of EPRIS Project Manager. The PPRO secretarial staff, Kathy Dorris, June Barrow, Deborah Peck, Helen Sandoz, Stephanie Smith, and Nancy Hood, typed and retyped the torrent of manuscripts that flowed from the project. Sincere thanks go to Nancy Brock for her diligent work placing the manuscripts for both volumes of this book on the computerized text editor, and performing uncountable editorial changes.

Kathleen King deserves special thanks for her careful and comprehensive editing, which contributed immeasurably to the readability and accuracy of the text.

Finally, we would like to express our gratitude to the National Science Foundation for supporting this project, and especially to our program managers, Dr. John Surmeier, Dr. Vaughn Blankenship, and Dr. Richard Mason. They were very helpful and exceedingly patient in the many phases of the project.

Despite the many contributions to this document, any errors or omissions herein are the responsibility of the authors.

Kenneth L. Kraemer
John L. King

VOLUME I

CONTENTS

83359

LIST OF FIGURES

1

INTRODUCTION:
LOCAL GOVERNMENTS,
INFORMATION, AND
COMPUTERS

This book provides policy guidance on the subject of computers in local government. It consists of two volumes. This volume, *A Manager's Guide*, presents an overview and summary of the major policy findings and recommendations taken from research and professional literature related to the use of computers in local governments. The second volume, *A Review of the Research*, presents a detailed review of research findings that form the basis of the policy recommendations presented in this volume. A reading of both volumes will provide a perspective on the whole field of computers and local governments.

Many management guides for computing have been written, but this differs from most in two respects. First, this book is written specifically for local governments. It draws from knowledge about computer use in all kinds of organizations, but it concentrates on local governments and their special characteristics. Second, this book is based upon empirical research and expert opinion, rather than simply on the knowledge of the authors. Thus, this book provides up-to-date advice drawn from the best of current knowledge about computers and information systems in local government.

The Setting: Local Governments Today

Over the last fifteen years, local governments have emerged as the fastest-growing sector of governmental activity in the United States. This interesting fact underscores one of the basic characteristics of local governments: they are fundamental building blocks of the federated governmental structure in this country. Despite the widespread media coverage of federal government expenditures and programs, the vast majority of citizen contacts with government take place at the local government level. Local governments provide almost all basic community services such as fire and police protection, parks and recreation, planning, and education. In addition, they are responsible for managing many programs such as welfare and health services mandated and funded by the federal or state governments. And in recent years, local governments have received authority and responsibility for a wider range of activities through programs such as revenue sharing.

The growth in local governments has been, in part, the result of population growth. Larger cities and counties need larger city and county governments. But population growth explains only a small part of the growth in local government. Much of the increase in local government activity has come from increased demands on local governments to deliver expanded services to citizens. At the same time, many local governments have come under considerable pressure to cut costs. Local governments, like other organizations, have been caught in an economic squeeze where prices and wages are increasing rapidly. Just to be able to perform the same services for the same costs, local governments must find ways of increasing productivity.

Local Governments, Productivity, and Information

Increases in productivity can come about through a variety of means, such as streamlining governmental operations, improving measures of service output to better control government activities, adopting new technologies and educational drives to encourage employees to be more cost conscious. The basic task of increasing productivity is to increase the efficiency of those local government operations that have substantial impact on other local government operations, thereby producing a high payoff for a relatively low investment. Comparatively inexpensive improvements in accounting, purchasing, and other management practices, for example, can save considerable amounts of money for local governments. And, with the proper guidance, many local governments have found that careful investment of reserve cash deposits can actually make money for the government treasury.

The key to improved productivity in local governments is improved control of local government planning and operations. Local governments essentially produce services rather than products, which makes it difficult for them to obtain improvements in productivity through mechanization. Unlike many businesses, local governments generally cannot hope to improve productivity through automation of production processes and increased use of special tools alone. Rather, they must rely on efforts to improve local planning and decision making, which will in turn result in better scheduling, staffing, purchasing, and management of local programs.

The common denominator of all planning and operational decisions is accurate, timely and relevant information. This is true whether the decisions be as routine as preparation of payroll checks, or as complex as consideration of a possible annexation of unincorporated territory. In addition, local governments are major repositories of important documentary information on citizens (birth, death, and marriage records, for example). Both the need for operational information and the mandated information-keeping activity show the importance of information to local governments. Clearly, improvement in the ability of local governments' ability to deal effectively with information would be a considerable step toward improved productivity.

Information and Computers

Computers have long been recognized as a major tool for improving the management and use of information in local governments. Many local governments now use computers, and many more are considering entering the field of computing. Computers have three basic characteristics that enable major improvements in management of information: they can process large volumes of data very quickly; they can perform processing activities time and again with unerring accuracy; and they can be programmed to use the same set of data in many different ways. These characteristics led first to application of computers to performing routine, repetitive data processing functions such as preparing payroll checks and utility bills. More recently, refinements in the technology have enabled extension of computing applications into more sophisticated activities, such as modeling, simulation, and planning.

Computers also have drawbacks. Like any other complex technology, computers must be adapted to the tasks they are to serve, and they must be managed efficiently and effectively if they are to produce benefits. A properly developed computer system that is conscientiously managed can prove a valuable cost-saving and service-improving tool for a local government. But an improperly developed computer system suffering under poor management can bring high costs and little payoff. It is important, therefore, that managers and policymakers in local governments understand what computers do, how they should be applied to organizational tasks, and how they should be organized and managed.

The Need for Direction

Many different kinds of technological advancements have been adopted by organizations in the past, the majority without the need for guidance by experts. For example, there were no national studies to provide guidance for use of typewriters, telephones, or photocopiers. Why, then, the concern about computers? There are two answers to this question. First, computers are by far the most complex modern technology to be widely adopted by use in local governments. Computers are very expensive, often constituting the most costly piece of equipment in a local government. Computing requires not only expensive equipment, but highly trained technical personnel to plan computer applications, write programs, and run the computer. Maintenance and continued development of computer-based systems create high ongoing costs. A fully functioning computer-based system also takes considerable time to plan and develop, often several years, and continues to evolve and expand once established. Most other technologies are simply installed and used, with a minimum of training for the users.

Second, computers offer much greater promise of assisting local governments than other technologies. Other technologies serve either a useful general purpose, such as telephones and copiers that facilitate communication among all users, or highly specific purposes in individual departments, as with a police radar unit. Computers, however, can potentially make very important contributions to the major planning, management, and operating functions of all local government departments. They can be programmed to perform simple, routine tasks such as printing bills; or they can be put to use calculating complex equations for traffic engineers or simulating population and development futures for planners. And many experts believe that future technological advancements will both expand the capabilities of computers and bring down their hardware cost.

Management's Role in Computing

The utility of computers is highly dependent on the people using them. Computer technology is complex and frequently mysterious to lay people, but it is still only a tool. Computers only do what they are designed and programmed to do, and then only if properly managed. Most modern computers are technically capable of performing impressive tasks, given proper development and programming. Yet, it is often argued that computers are underutilized or applied to the wrong tasks. Most of the serious problems in computing can be traced back to people. It is people who make improper selections of computer hardware for the job at hand. It is people who make mistakes in establishing development priorities for development of computer applications. It is people who fail to manage computer technology in a sensible, effective manner.

A brief examination of the development of computing in local governments reveals the importance of this human element. Computer use has evolved in local governments, beginning in the largest governments and applied to the most routine processing tasks. Over time, a larger number of governments have adopted the technology, and an increasing number of tasks have successfully been automated. Yet, this evolution has been characterized by great inconsistency in the kinds of experiences different governments have had with computing. Some governments have succeeded in developing high-quality data processing at a reasonable cost and in a very short time. Others have had unfortunate experiences with data processing, plagued by high costs, missed deadlines, and small payoffs. Since the technology from one government to another varies little, these differences in success must stem from differences in approaches to development and management of the technology.

This evolution within local governments is easy to trace. Generally, each local government department gathers the data it needs to support its own activities and make its own decisions. Thus, with the exception of special requests of top management, the collection and use of data for information purposes is usually based on departmental organization, tradition, and technology. Computers were first applied to the most logical and easily automated functions, particularly financial and accounting tasks, which usually take place in the finance department. Thus, computers were first used and housed in finance departments in local governments. Over time, the technology improved and local governments became more familiar with computers, which led to increased use of computing for a variety of tasks throughout other departments. Today, most local government computer activities bear the mark of this evolution. Financial applications, and often the finance department, dominate use of the computer. Other departments lag in use of the technology. Most important, computer applications still tend to concentrate on meeting the narrow needs of specific departmental activities.

The Need for Information Management

Over the last several years, researchers and experts on local government computing have argued that two major reorientations should take place in development and use of computer technology. First, they have recommended that local governments integrate and standardize their data-processing activities in order to make it possible to use one or a few large data bases for all government data needs. Second, they have argued that data gathered for operational purposes also be formatted and processed in such a way that they are available for management purposes. In other words, these experts have recommended that government data resources be consolidated and organized in such a way to serve both management and planning needs of the local government. This concept has come to be called "information management."

Under the information management concept, a local government would (1) define a data base that satisfies operational and planning-management information needs; (2) rationalize the data flows throughout the local government to provide for these information needs; (3) automate appropriate data into a data base, and coordinate the operations that furnish and update those data; (4) insure that users have a highly flexible computer capability that allows for processing, computation, and retrieval of data. This concept is simple in theory, but it has proven much more difficult to implement than anticipated

due to the complexity of local government operations and their data requirements, the still-emerging state of the technology, and a lack of practical
knowledge about how to build systems around the information management
concept.

Today, therefore, there exists a gap between what conceivably can be done
with the technology and what is actually being done. Indeed, some argue that
the concept of information management can never be reached in perfection.
But even if this is true, it remains sensible to strive toward filling the gap and
developing optimal use of computer technology in local governments. This
book was prepared to help local governments fill that gap.

The Relevance of Research

Given that the information management concept is a desirable goal for
local government data processing, the problem that remains is how to convey
to local governments the necessary sound guidance to help them develop their
computer systems in a way consistent with the concept. This is where research
findings make a most important contribution.

The obvious advantage of using research findings as a guide over people's
opinions is that research findings have been derived from objective analysis of
test situations or real-world observations. Research findings are less likely to
be biased toward one point of view or another. In short, research findings
frequently are more reliable as bases of action than are people's opinions. For
that reason, this book is based wherever possible on research data and findings.
Where opinion enters, it is the considered opinion of acknowledged experts in
particular relevant fields, and it is noted as such.

The Policy Perspective

The key to successful development and use of computing in local governments is proper policy for computing. No local government manager can
adequately handle all computing tasks himself, and many managers do not
have the time to deal directly with computing at all. It is necessary, therefore,
to establish policies that will guide the development and use of computing to
serve the needs of departments, management, and the local government generally. Since the task of developing and managing use of computing is complex,
it is helpful to note the major concerns a local government manager should
be aware of. There are six major concerns:

  1. The purpose and role of the data processing function in the local
  government.
  2. The organization and management of data processing operations.
  3. Financial considerations in establishing and developing computing.

4. The human and organizational impacts of computing, particularly as related to personnel matters.

5. Proper selection and use of computer equipment and technology.

6. The requirements for data confidentiality and privacy, in light of the need for proper disclosure and open government.

These concerns reflect the operational dimensions of the information management concept. The more carefully and comprehensively these major concerns are dealt with in forming policy for development and use of computing, the more likely the information management concept can be approximated.

Using This Book

This book is organized as a logical progression, from background information on computing, through initial policy concerns for dealing with computer systems, to the human impacts of computing, the potentials of new technology, and social concerns such as privacy. The background is provided by Chapters 2 and 3, which detail the evolution of computer use in local governments and the state of that use today. These chapters include discussion of the various concepts for computer usage, the experiences of local governments with these concepts, current patterns of computer use among governments, roadblocks to sophisticated use of computing, and probable future trends in computer use.

Chapter 4 covers the major issues and policy concerns in the area of planning and management of data processing activity. This includes issues such as alternatives for procurement of computing capability, organization and location of the computing function within the local government structure, the role of top management in computing decisions, the major organizational impacts of computing that concern the manager, and a number of management concerns involving design, development, and installation security.

Chapter 5 deals with financial aspects of computing in local government. Covered are such topics as financial evaluation of procurement alternatives, methods of financing computer operations, investment strategies for developing computer operations, cost-benefit analysis, mechanisms for allocating computing resources among users, use of charging schemes, and methods for accounting for computer use among users.

Chapter 6 covers the personnel and manpower issues involved in computing. This includes topics such as the impact of computers on employment, job tasks, and employee attitudes, as well as a thorough discussion of personnel policies related to computing such as recruitment, training, promotion, wage and salary structures, and the interface between computer and non-computer personnel.

Chapter 7 deals with the major new issues in computer technology that local governments should be aware of. It covers system building procedures, development of data base management and related systems, geoprocessing, and distributed computing.

Chapter 8 addresses the important topic of privacy and disclosure as related to computer systems in local government. It includes discussion of the major threats to privacy computerized personal records can bring, contrasts the need for privacy with the need for open and candid disclosure of information required by open government, explores the meaning of federal and state privacy legislation for local governments, and recommends a course of action local managers can take to avoid privacy problems.

Chapter 9 discusses urban information systems as a field of study, and explores some problems facing further study in the field. Following Chapter 9 are a short bibliography of key works a manager can read to become more familiar with the field of urban information systems, together with a list of the other works on information systems from PPRO; a glossary of computer-related terms a manager is likely to come in contact with; and a brief biography of the authors.

It is recommended that the book be read through from beginning to end, like a novel. In this way the reader will be able to follow the progression of issues and ideas from the general case of computers in local governments, through topics of policy concern related to computing, and back to consideration of the impacts of computers on social issues such as privacy.

2

THE EVOLUTION
OF COMPUTER USE
IN LOCAL
GOVERNMENTS

The use of automation to assist in the task of managing government records began in the late 19th century, when the first mechanical unit-record processing machines were introduced. Use of electronic data processing equipment (EDP), in turn, began relatively recently in the mid-1950s. This chapter documents the evolution of electronic data processing use in local government from that period until the present.

The Role of Information Systems in Local Government

Before discussing the different ways computers have been applied to the task of data management in local governments, it will be useful to identify the role information systems play in government and, correspondingly, the role computers play in information systems. The topic of information systems is commonly entwined with discussion of computers, but computers and information systems are not the same. There are many kinds of information systems that rely on manual methods of data collection, processing, and storage. Even if a particular information system utilizes computers, the computer is only a part of the total system. Computers are usually applied only to the tasks of storing and processing data, but an information system goes beyond storage and processing of data, and uses tools besides computers to accomplish its primary task of bringing together data items to form information for some decision or action. Figure 1 shows the major activities involved in management of data from source to end use.

The first activity is data collection--an activity that involves more people than any other information activity, since data are collected from many places and many people, often from citizens themselves. Second, there is data organization, which pulls relevant data together into files by particular class, such

FIGURE 1
General Information System Model

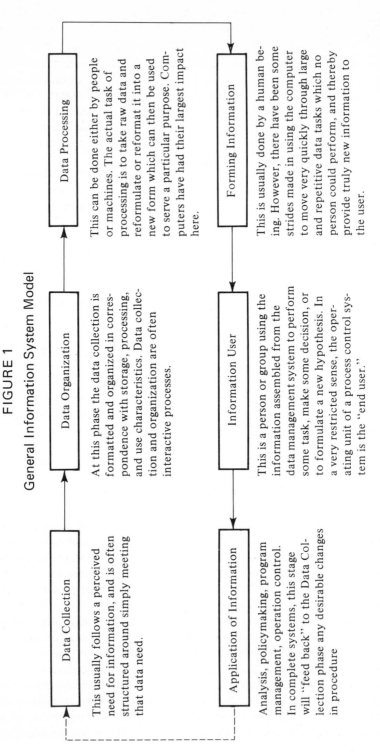

Data Collection

This usually follows a perceived need for information, and is often structured around simply meeting that data need.

Data Organization

At this phase the data collection is formatted and organized in correspondence with storage, processing, and use characteristics. Data collection and organization are often interactive processes.

Data Processing

This can be done either by people or machines. The actual task of processing is to take raw data and reformulate or reformat it into a new form which can then be used to serve a particular purpose. Computers have had their largest impact here.

Forming Information

This is usually done by a human being. However, there have been some strides made in using the computer to move very quickly through large and repetitive data tasks which no person could perform, and thereby provide truly new information to the user.

Information User

This is a person or group using the information assembled from the data management system to perform some task, make some decision, or to formulate a new hypothesis. In a very restricted sense, the operating unit of a process control system is the "end user."

Application of Information

Analysis, policymaking, program management, operation control. In complete systems, this stage will "feed back" to the Data Collection phase any desirable changes in procedure

Source: K. L. Kraemer, and J. L. King, *Computers Power and Urban Management: What Every Local Executive Should Know.* Sage Professional Papers in Administrative and Policy Studies. Vol. 1, Series 03–031, 1976.

as arrest records, dog licenses, and taxable properties. Third is data processing where data stored in files are screened for particular characteristics, linked to other data, and manipulated to conform to some desired output such as a payroll list or a management report. The final activity is the forming of information from data and using it. At this level, data from the data processing phase are reviewed for information content and relevance and are used in some way to resolve the situation for which they were intended.

These four activities constitute an "information system," and the purpose of an information system is to bring data together from a variety of sources to form information. The coordination and control of these information system activities is called "information management." The ideal state of information management in local government consists of bringing relevant data elements together to form information suited to answering particular questions for the management of community affairs.

The following discussion of the major approaches to computer use in local government utilizes the classification of activities presented in Figure 1 to indicate how each approach differs from the others.

Local Government Approaches to Computer Use

There are five general approaches toward use of computers in local governments. These can be referred to as the housekeeping approach, the databank approach, the model building approach, the process control approach, and the integrated systems approach. Figure 2 shows the appearance of these approaches over the last 20 years.

The Housekeeping Approach

The housekeeping approach is essentially a transfer of manual record-keeping procedures to machine automation. Conversion to automation is basically a mechanical problem. It emphasizes sorting, counting, and simple arithmetic operations. Examples of housekeeping applications are computerized utility billing, payroll accounting, tax accounting, real property record-keeping, and voter registration.

As Figure 3 shows, the primary emphasis of the housekeeping approach is on data processing. Its goal is to automate simple, repetitive elements of data processing operations to enable faster and more accurate manipulation of record information. There is very little emphasis on data collection or organization, since actual processing is carried out within the same context that existed with the manual system. However, there is often an attempt to standardize data formats and input procedures to meet the requirements of machine processing. The housekeeping approach has little impact on the process

FIGURE 2

The Appearance of Local Government Approaches to Computer Use

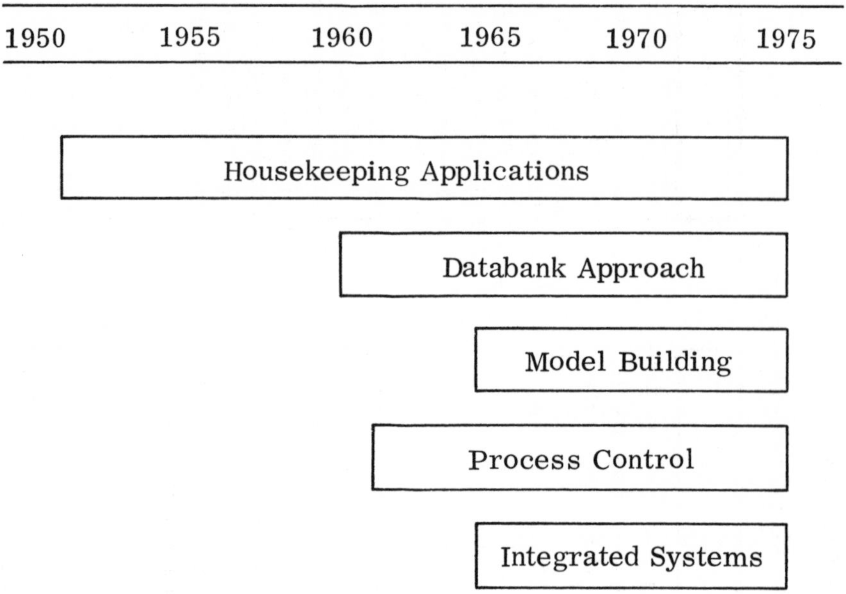

1950	1955	1960	1965	1970	1975

Housekeeping Applications

Databank Approach

Model Building

Process Control

Integrated Systems

Source: Compiled by the authors.

of actually converting data to information, or on the user's interaction with that information. Usually, automation improves the speed of processing and accuracy of records, but these are mainly operational improvements that may not greatly alter the overall information activities in the organization.

Housekeeping applications are by far the most common computer applications in local government. They were the first to be developed, and in general remain the most practical applications of the technology. Local governments adopting use of computer technology usually exploit housekeeping applications first, and wait until they are running smoothly before expanding computer use into more complicated tasks such as analysis and management support.

The Databank Approach

A databank is a centralized storehouse of data that can be applied to multiple information needs. The primary emphasis of the databank approach

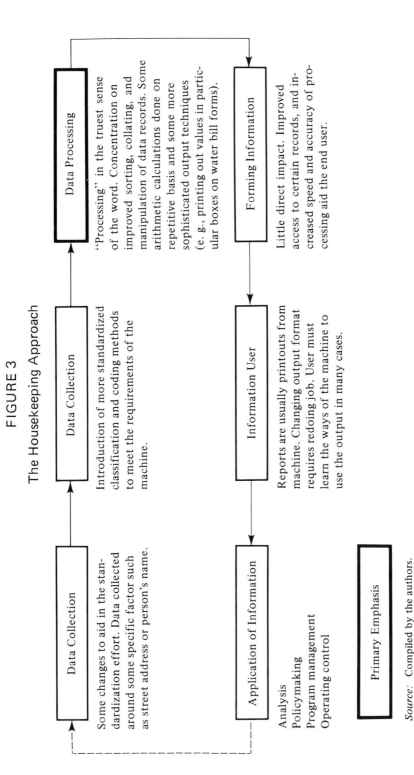

FIGURE 3

The Housekeeping Approach

Data Collection

Some changes to aid in the standardization effort. Data collected around some specific factor such as street address or person's name.

Data Collection

Introduction of more standardized classification and coding methods to meet the requirements of the machine.

Data Processing

"Processing" in the truest sense of the word. Concentration on improved sorting, collating, and manipulation of data records. Some arithmetic calculations done on repetitive basis and some more sophisticated output techniques (e. g., printing out values in particular boxes on water bill forms).

Forming Information

Little direct impact. Improved access to certain records, and increased speed and accuracy of processing aid the end user.

Information User

Reports are usually printouts from machine. Changing output format requires redoing job. User must learn the ways of the machine to use the output in many cases.

Application of Information

Analysis
Policymaking
Program management
Operating control

Primary Emphasis

Source: Compiled by the authors.

13

is on data organization, as shown in Figure 4. The early proponents of the databank asserted that much of the data collected in day-to-day routine operations could be shared on a government-wide basis, thereby reducing duplicate collection and storage of data, and could be used for planning-management as well as operations thereby increasing the multiple use of data. They recommended establishment of a data pool or "bank" that would be manipulated by a general program language to allow for analysis, processing, and reporting activities. With a databank, a government would possess a massive, retrievable data file that would be updated by operating agencies and continuously available to a wide variety of users. Examples of early databank projects include the Tulsa Metropolitan Data Center Project and the Pittsburgh Community Renewal Program, both of which were primarily oriented toward planning uses, and the Alexandria, Virginia Databank and the Portland Metropolitan Databank which were intended for more general governmental use.

The secondary emphases of the databank approach are increases in amount and kinds of data collected and more standardization in the data collection phase. There is often greater need for data management software in the processing phase, and some added flexibility to the user due to availability of more relevant data for each information need. Perhaps the strongest secondary emphasis of the databank approach is on the conversion of data to information. The databank implicitly requires sharing of data among separate departments, and provides for storage of data that have no immediate use, but which might be called on at a later time.

At the time of this writing, there are no existing government-wide databanks of the kind envisioned by the first proponents of this approach, although specialized, one-time databanks frequently exist using, for example, census data or land use data. The early databanks failed primarily because they required data to be collected by one department to be used by other departments or top management without specific use for the collecting department, and because many of the data collection efforts were not tied to the routine information-handling activities of the departments but were imposed as additional requirements without commensurable benefits. It was found that the cost of gathering and storing massive amounts of data that were not destined for a specific use was prohibitive. In addition, it became clear that the task of managing huge data files to answer a few specific questions was a laborious task with little payoff. It was easier in many cases to rely on the older method of gathering data for answering questions as needed.

The Model-Building Approach

The model-building approach uses the powerful computational capability of the computer to perform simulation and modeling of real-world situations

FIGURE 4

The Databank Approach

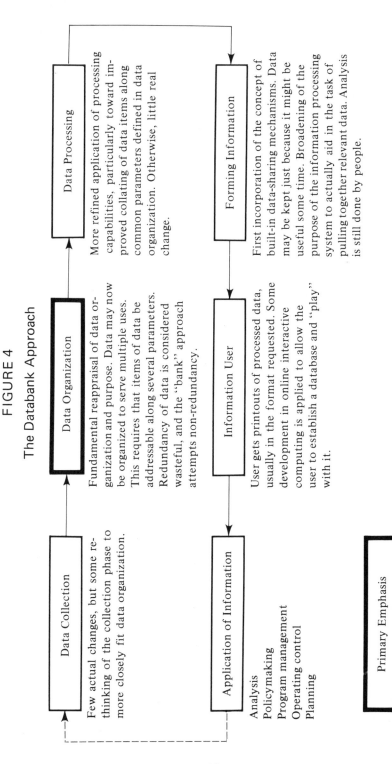

Source: Compiled by the authors.

15

for planning, management, and research purposes. The model-building approach is different from the housekeeping and databank approaches in that it does not necessarily draw on operational data from the local government. It can use "artificial" data to explore the likely outcomes from different hypothetical conditions. As shown in Figure 5, the main emphases of modeling are on processing data and forming information. The model-building approach depends on the power of the computer to manipulate large amounts of data in a short period of time. In a sense, model-building attempts to build "new" information from the computer by exploiting its speed and computational capabilities to perform multiple, complex data manipulation that a person could never (or would never) perform. There are few other emphases of the model-building approach.

Early model-building efforts grew out of the need to simulate urban and environmental problems for analysis purposes. These simulations were computer-driven models incorporating many variables such as population, housing supply and demand, air quality, and employment statistics. By constructing models based on these data, then changing input parameters, it was hoped that the simulations would offer insight into the dynamic nature of urban and environmental problems. Examples of these early model-building approaches are the San Francisco Housing Model, the Land Use Model for Southeastern Wisconsin, and the Urban Dynamics Models. Model-building was also applied to the task of educating future urban managers through interactive games such as METRO-APEX and the Community Land Use Game.

The elaborate model-building exercises have not had the hoped-for impacts. It is much more difficult to successfully model urban environments than the early proponents anticipated, and the models never reached the theoretical or operational refinement necessary for major contributions to local government planning and management. However, recent applications of computer-based model building have proven promising. These applications are more modest in scope and more practical in design. Usually, they are intended to assist in planning for specific projects such as deployment of service vehicles, arrangement of police beats, routing of public transportation, and location of municipal facilities such as fire stations or parks.

The Process Control Approach

The process control approach utilizes computer technology to control continuous or repetitive operations like traffic signals, water and electrical utility lines, heating and air conditioning systems, and emergency vehicle dispatching. The main emphases of process control are on data collection and on actual use of information, as shown in Figure 6. The purpose of the process control approach is to improve efficiency and reduce the amount of human

FIGURE 5
The Model-Building Approach

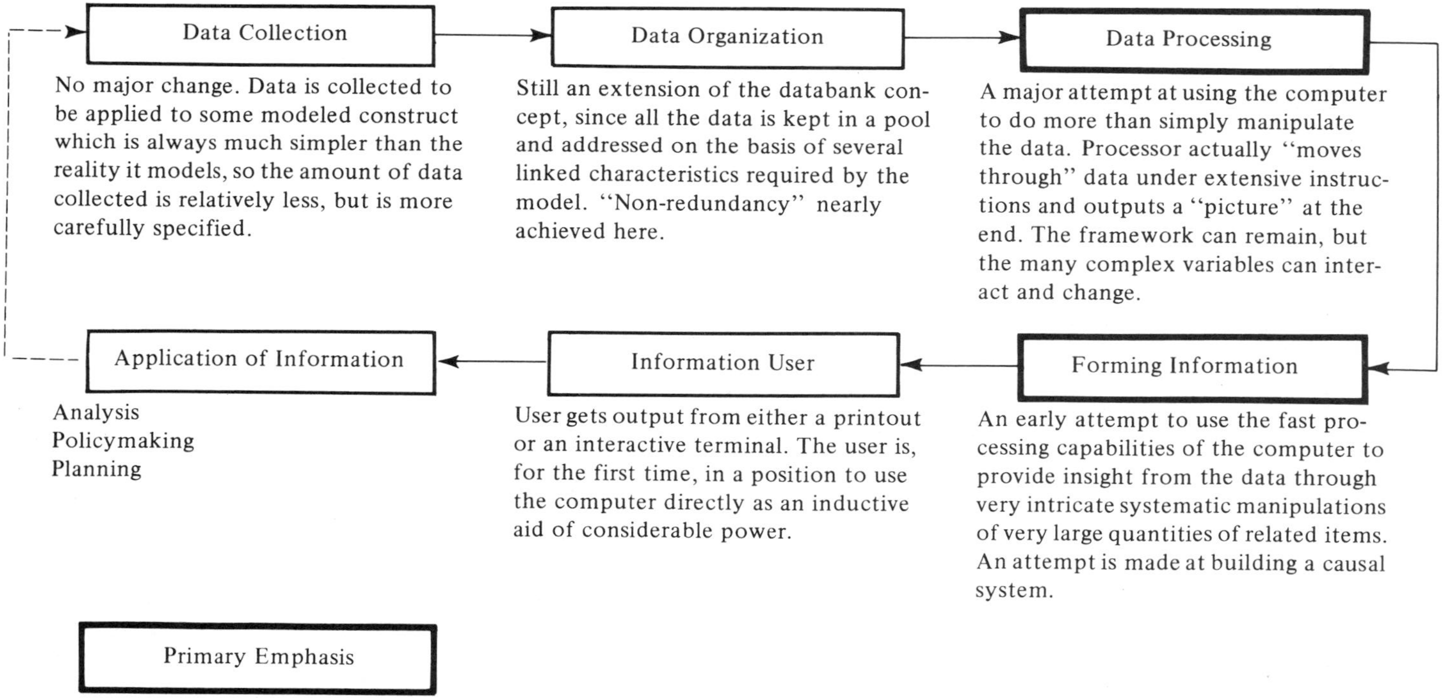

Data Collection

No major change. Data is collected to be applied to some modeled construct which is always much simpler than the reality it models, so the amount of data collected is relatively less, but is more carefully specified.

Data Organization

Still an extension of the databank concept, since all the data is kept in a pool and addressed on the basis of several linked characteristics required by the model. "Non-redundancy" nearly achieved here.

Data Processing

A major attempt at using the computer to do more than simply manipulate the data. Processor actually "moves through" data under extensive instructions and outputs a "picture" at the end. The framework can remain, but the many complex variables can interact and change.

Forming Information

An early attempt to use the fast processing capabilities of the computer to provide insight from the data through very intricate systematic manipulations of very large quantities of related items. An attempt is made at building a causal system.

Information User

User gets output from either a printout or an interactive terminal. The user is, for the first time, in a position to use the computer directly as an inductive aid of considerable power.

Application of Information

Analysis
Policymaking
Planning

Primary Emphasis

Source: Compiled by the authors.

17

attention required by certain mechanical operations. Process control incorporates advanced sensing technology to provide a direct link between data collection and the processing phase. An increasingly common example of process control is use of remote surface sensors in streets to measure traffic flow and coordinate traffic signals. The application of information is immediate and direct, usually by-passing any human "users," and going straight to the controls of the process as feedback.

The process control approach does not emphasize the data organization, conversion of data to information, or the human "user" phases of the information system. Data are "organized" by the hardwired linkages between collection devices and processors. There is no conversion of data to information in the normal sense because the output primarily serves to guide and control the process in operation. The goal of process control is to minimize the need for human monitoring. However, this does not mean process control has no spinoff to human users. The advancements in sensing and controls technology have enabled human operators to collect "up to the minute" accounts of conditions by way of recording mechanisms attached to processors. In this way a human capability of analyzing broader problems (e.g., traffic patterns on particular streets over time) may be enhanced.

Examples of process control can now be seen in many cities. Most large public utilities now use computer-assisted monitoring devices to regulate distribution and flow of gas, electricity, and water, and to enact emergencyy measures when needed. Traffic control through automated signals like those in Toronto, and freeway monitoring systems such as those in Los Angeles, are becoming more common all the time. Highly sophisticated applications of control technology, such as in the Bay Area Rapid Transit System in California, are now in development or operation.

The Integrated Systems Approach

The integrated systems approach views the entire flow of data and information within an organization as a system in itself. Proponents of this approach contend that the success of an information system design rests on a thorough analysis of the way data flow within the organization and the uses to which they are put. By understanding such data flows and uses, an information system can be built that will meet the information needs of the local government more efficiently and effectively than otherwise. In addition, it is argued that such integrated systems are more versatile and useful than a set of small, "stand alone" systems. The integrated systems approach concentrates on data sharing and centralization of the data management activity to promote efficiency and effectiveness.

The primary emphases of the integrated system approach are on forming a comprehensive data management activity that includes collection, organiza-

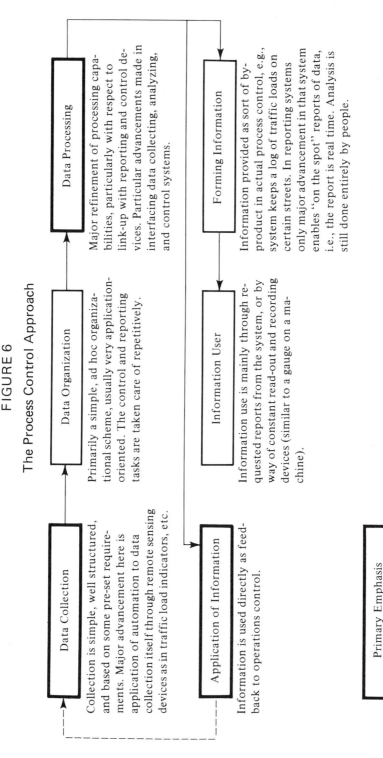

FIGURE 6

The Process Control Approach

Data Collection

Collection is simple, well structured, and based on some pre-set requirements. Major advancement here is application of automation to data collection itself through remote sensing devices as in traffic load indicators, etc.

Data Organization

Primarily a simple, ad hoc organizational scheme, usually very application-oriented. The control and reporting tasks are taken care of repetitively.

Data Processing

Major refinement of processing capabilities, particularly with respect to link-up with reporting and control devices. Particular advancements made in interfacing data collecting, analyzing, and control systems.

Forming Information

Information provided as sort of by-product in actual process control, e.g. system keeps a log of traffic loads on certain streets. In reporting systems only major advancement in that system enables "on the spot" reports of data, i.e., the report is real time. Analysis is still done entirely by people.

Information User

Information use is mainly through requested reports from the system, or by way of constant read-out and recording devices (similar to a gauge on a machine).

Application of Information

Information is used directly as feedback to operations control.

Primary Emphasis

Source: Compiled by the authors.

19

tion and processing of data, and on forging a feedback link from information applications to the data management activity as shown in Figure 7. All data management operations (collection, organization, and processing) are integrated to facilitate meeting multiple user needs, and the user acts as a link in the system by interacting directly with the computer and the data management staff.

Indirectly, the integrated systems approach concentrates upon the data conversion phase by emphasizing data sharing and frequent updating of files to assure accuracy. The user in an integrated system interacts with the machine through a remote terminal, and makes requests of decision-oriented data from the integrated data base.

The integrated systems approach is best exemplifed by the Integrated Municipal Information System (IMIS) concept. There have been several attempts to build IMIS, such as the IBM-New Haven project, the Santa Clara County, California, LOGIC project, and the Urban Information Systems Interagency Committee (USAC) projects sponsored by the federal government through the Department of Housing and Urban Development. Of these, only the USAC projects at Charlotte, North Carolina, and Wichita Falls, Texas, have actually attempted a full scale, start-to-finish integrated system. To date, none of the integrated municipal information projects has resulted in a fully operational municipal-wide system, although portions of such a system have been built and may provide proof of concept.

In contrast to building integrated systems from the ground up, several local governments have attempted to build partially integrated systems by selecting data needed for management and planning out of operational files. This is usually done by writing special software routines that "sift" the desired data out of existing applications files, and aggregate these data into a new file. This new file then provides a base for analysis that will help planning and management. Examples of this approach can be seen in Lane County, Oregon, in the Los Angeles Community Analysis Bureau, and in the Forecast Analysis Center of Orange County, California. Less extensive versions of this approach can be found in a number of medium and large sized local governments. The advantage of this "after the fact" approach to an integrated system is that the government can realize many of the benefits of an integrated system without having to undertake the very costly and time-consuming task of building a new system or drastically changing an old system.

A Perspective on This Evolution

The approaches toward application of computer technology to local government operations illustrate the general evolution of computer use in local governments. The evolution has been both directed and undirected. It has been directed in the sense that there has been widespread agreement that the poten-

FIGURE 7

The Integrated Systems Approach

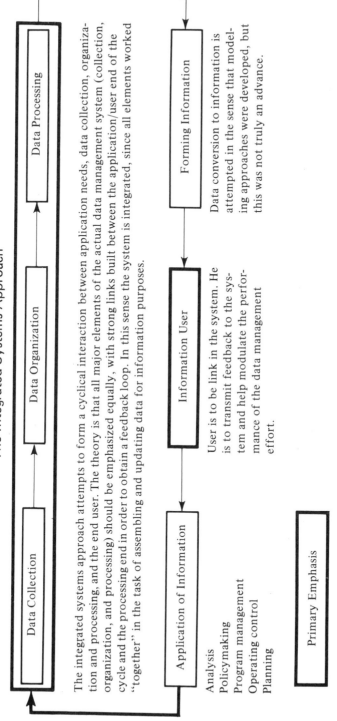

| Data Collection | → | Data Organization | → | Data Processing |

The integrated systems approach attempts to form a cyclical interaction between application needs, data collection, organization and processing, and the end user. The theory is that all major elements of the actual data management system (collection, organization, and processing) should be emphasized equally, with strong links built between the application/user end of the cycle and the processing end in order to obtain a feedback loop. In this sense the system is integrated, since all elements worked "together" in the task of assembling and updating data for information purposes.

Forming Information

Data conversion to information is attempted in the sense that modeling approaches were developed, but this was not truly an advance.

Information User

User is to be link in the system. He is to transmit feedback to the system and help modulate the performance of the data management effort.

Application of Information

Analysis
Policymaking
Program management
Operating control
Planning

Primary Emphasis

Source: Compiled by the authors.

tial of the technology should be exploited, yet undirected in that development of actual applications has been spread over identifying and exploring many specialized uses.

It is useful to think of these approaches to computer use as experiments. Some experiments have paid off and are reflected in approaches still in use, as in the case of housekeeping applications. Others have not paid off and have either been abandoned or drastically modified in concept, as with databanks and model building. Still others are relative newcomers that show promise for the future, such as process control applications and integrated systems. As time goes on, the success or failure of these newer approaches will become more evident, and they will be abandoned or continued. Similarly, new approaches to use will certainly emerge.

There is one important conclusion to be drawn from this discussion of the evolution of computer use in local governments: computers have been adopted and developed in local governments as a joint function of the capabilities of available technology, the needs of local government, and the ability of people to apply the technology to meet those needs. Thus, it is not surprising that attempts to apply the technology have varied over time with changes and improvements in the technology and in concepts for applying it. Similarly, as individuals and organizations have become more experienced and knowledgeable about how the technology can and cannot be of service to local government, the approaches to use have become more refined. The next chapter discusses current profiles and trends in use of computers in local government.

3

PROFILES
AND TRENDS IN
COMPUTER USE

Current Use of Computers in Local Government

More than half of all U.S. cities and counties over 10,000 population use computers in one way or another. The extent of computer use among local governments is directly related to size of local governments as measured by population. Nearly all the largest local governments have adopted computers, whereas the smallest local governments are still in the process of adopting the technology. The larger local governments (those over 100,000 population) began to adopt computers in the early 1960s, and today about 75 percent of these governments use computers. The smaller governments (10,000-25,000) began to adopt in the very late 1960s and early 1970s, and today show a computer use rate of about 50 percent. As time goes on, it is likely that the medium and smaller sized local governments will catch up with the larger governments in extent of computer use.

Investment in computing among local governments is about 1 percent of annual operating budget per year. This figure varies somewhat by size of government, with smaller governments spending approximately .5 percent of their operating budgets and larger governments slightly over 1 percent. Counties spend slightly more proportionately than do cities, perhaps due to the fact that many county operations such as health and welfare require extensive record-keeping activities. It should be noted that these figures reflect only the direct expenditures on computing, including hardware, software, maintenance, and EDP staff. They do not reflect the EDP-related costs of user departments. If these were taken into account, the total average EDP expenditure could be as high as 2 percent of operating budgets.

The level of computing capability available in local governments varies, as one would expect, with local government size and level of investment in

EDP. In general, larger local governments have more computing capability than smaller governments. Some larger governments have more than one large computer mainframe, and most have larger core and on-line storage and make greater use of time-sharing. Medium and smaller sized local governments that have computers of their own usually have only one mainframe with small or medium core capacity and batch processing.

Personnel devoted to EDP operations average less than 1 percent of total local government personnel, regardless of size. Thus, the size of an EDP staff varies proportionately with the size of the government. In all cases, about 25 percent of EDP personnel are analysts and programmers. EDP staff size in user departments is usually smaller than staff size in the EDP department itself.

Arrangements for Use of Computers

There are several ways local governments can procure computing capability. These alternatives will be discussed in detail in later chapters. In general, most large local governments do their own computing in-house on rented or leased equipment. In contrast, a majority of smaller governments do their computing out-of-house by using service bureaus or cooperative facilities with other local governments. Of those smaller local governments that do computing in-house, most own their own computer.

Among all governments that do computing in-house, the computing activity is frequently located in the finance department. This is to be expected, for the first uses of computing usually occur in the finance department, and financial applications of computing often make the greatest demands on computer resources. Nevertheless, there is a trend to move the computing activity out of the finance department and into an independent EDP department. This trend appears most strongly in larger governments, and is in part the result of increasing use of the computer for non-finance applications. As the use of the computer moves beyond traditional finance oriented tasks into new departmental operations, there is pressure to move the computing capability into an independent organizational position that gives all users equal access.

Applications of Computers

Most applications of computers in local governments involve automation of routine housekeeping tasks. About three-fourths of all applications in local governments are for record-keeping, calculating and printing tasks associated with housekeeping operations. The remaining one-fourth of the computer applications are spread over more sophisticated uses of the computer, such as information retrieval from databases, process control, and analysis tasks involving integration of different data.

Of the routine housekeeping applications of computers, most are in the area of accounting and financial control. These include taxation, accounting, assessment, utility billing, and payroll preparation. Following financial applications, the next most common uses of the computer are for routine tasks in law enforcement, courts, and budget and management. These areas are not only the most common uses of computing among local governments, but are the most extensively developed applications within local governments as well.

The reasons behind the predominance of housekeeping applications are easy to see: these applications are relatively straightforward and simple; they are tailored to specific and definable tasks; they do not have to be modified frequently; and they are fairly inexpensive to develop compared to more sophisticated applications. Housekeeping applications, on the whole, offer a high payoff for a relatively small investment. This investment-payoff argument is also applied to sophisticated applications, only with the premise that initial costs and final payoffs are greater. Why, then, are there so few sophisticated applications? The answer to this question deserves special consideration.

Roadblocks to Sophisticated Computer Use

The primary blocks to use of sophisticated computer applications in local governments are mainly due to problems of development and transfer. There are four major problems local governments face when seeking to develop or transfer-in sophisticated applications. First, most sophisticated applications are very difficult to develop. They are usually complex, thus requiring elaborate systems analysis and programming. Complex programs are usually more difficult to bring up to operational performance, and require extensive debugging. With all these difficulties facing development of a sophisticated application, there may be little incentive to abandon traditional methods of information management, even if they are cumbersome, in favor of an automated system of uncertain utility and reliability. Prototype applications developed as examples in selected sites might demonstrate that a certain application concept is feasible, but such applications are difficult to transfer to other governments.

A second major factor is the prohibitive cost for developing sophisticated computer applications. If a development effort for a new application places extraordinary demands on EDP staff and user personnel, the costs in both money and time may be great. Again, the concept of transferring sophisticated applications from one government to another holds the promise of obtaining sophisticated computer capability at lower costs, but transfer projects often incur higher costs than expected. Since the application being brought in was originally developed for another local setting, it might not be compatible with the transferee's equipment, procedures, or needs. Also, such transferred applications must be brought up on the transferee's system, and this requires the time and attention of programmers, analysts, users, and data processing management.

A third problem with the development of sophisticated applications of the technology has been the result of poor computer acquisition and development procedures often employed by local governments. Many local governments, and particularly those adopting computers for the first time, are unsure how to go about procuring a computer system that will really meet their needs. There is a great deal of difference in capability, even among the range of machines offered by one computer vendor. Procurement of a machine too limited for the tasks a local government wants to automate usually leads to upgrading the machine. This disrupts the development cycle, and especially the development of sophisticated applications since the needed housekeeping applications must first be transferred to the new machine and made operational. If a machine with too much capacity is purchased, there is often a desire to "fill up" the slack capacity so it will not appear that the machine is underutilized. This can result in establishment of applications that really are not needed by the government, but that become entrenched. If this happens, it may be difficult to dislodge these low-utility applications when the more sophisticated applications are being developed. This, in turn, may lead to desire for a larger machine to handle the exaggerated demand. The point of this is simple: the procurement of computer capability should be tied to the desire to develop specific applications over a particular period of time.

The final problem in developing sophisticated applications is actually corollary to those above. It is a simple fact that many local governments lack personnel with sufficient training and skill to deal with the problems sophisticated applications development brings. Highly qualified computer specialists are relatively rare, and specialists who know the needs of local governments and the problems of developing sophisticated applications are even rarer. Large cities and counties can usually hire the talent they need because they have sufficient scale of operations to justify paying high salaries. Smaller local governments, unfortunately, are usually more constrained by finances.

The State of the Art in Perspective

Given these problems, it is easy to see why computer use in local governments consists largely of automation applied to routine operations that were formerly done manually. In some cases, even these simple computerized operations are not performed very well (there is more than one local government with an inadequate payroll processing system). Sophisticated applications of the technology are concentrated primarily in larger local governments. Among smaller local governments, one may have an advanced automated booking system in its police department, and little else. Another may have a voter registration system, and little else. Computer technology is being used by a majority of local governments, but there is little continuity in sophistication or quality of computer applications.

The expression "state of the art" is an accurate reflection of this field. Computer use in many local governments is still more an art than an operational science. Some local governments have made impressive use of the technology, while comparable governments have had great difficulty reaching their data processing objectives within budgetary constraints. Presumably, those governments with highly successful computer operations are successful because they have developed their operations with a "proper mix" of financial, intellectual, managerial, and technical resources. Research into what makes for a "proper mix" of these resources is now underway, but until the results of such research are available, the field will remain primarily an artistic endeavor.

Where the Evolution is Likely to Go

Like most developmental processes, computer use in local governments has grown through a sequence of trials and errors. The applications of the past 20 years, in spite of their shortcomings, have shown one fact: computing technology can offer substantial benefits in the present, if properly utilized and managed, and holds even greater potential for the future as problems are worked out.

Roadblocks to sophisticated applications are due to shortcomings in both the technology and in human factors. With each step toward greater computing capability, there has been a subsequent increase in the need for better understanding of how people use information. In the same way that the technology of the automobile has caused policymakers and planners to reconsider the broader purposes of transportation systems, the technology of data processing has spurred new thinking about the role of information in management of human affairs. This kind of rethinking is essential to future refinement of both the technology and the uses made of it.

In the meantime, that is, until the major problems are solved, the task facing the policymaker is to use currently available technology to the best level allowed by current knowledge. This does not necessarily mean using the most advanced computers coupled to the most advanced applications software. To do so would entail living on the leading edge of the technology, which is a very expensive and often risky way to live. For some local governments, the risks and expense are worthwhile, and through the innovative efforts of those governments the whole field of computer use in local governments moves forward. Still, there are obvious advantages to reliance on proven, albeit less exciting technology: primarily lower costs and greater overall reliability of outcomes.

For most local governments, the possible payoffs of being innovative probably are not worth the extra costs, and the wise course is to rely on proven technology.

In any case, whether the technology is commonplace or right off the designer's drawing board, the important thing is to put it to work facilitating the way information is used in the organization for planning and management purposes. The following chapters of this book offer guidance that will assist in development of effective local government computing.

4

PLANNING AND
MANAGEMENT POLICY

This chapter discusses the key aspects of planning and managing computer-based information systems in local government. It is of particular importance to chief executives and department managers in local governments that make use of EDP, or are considering adopting EDP. The need for effective planning and management is agreed upon, and nearly every organization makes some attempt at it, but the actual process of planning and managing is more important, more complex, and more difficult than many realize.

In a sense, ultimate success or failure of an organization's use of computerized systems can be traced back to decisions made during planning or management. Decisions about computer-based information systems involve many factors, and are often made on the basis of imperfect information. This makes the decision process difficult and cumbersome, and the reliability of decisions somewhat risky. But it is possible to reduce this risk considerably by carefully covering as many key aspects of each decision as possible before reaching a conclusion.

An executive's greatest tool is the authority to insist on having as much good, relevant information as possible before making an important decision concerning an information system. This is true not only during planning, but also during operations where many critical decisions arise.[1] The following findings and conclusions from research on computerized information systems will help executives ask appropriate questions and push for complete and informed answers.[2]

---

[1]See *Computer, Power, and Urban Management: What Every Local Executive Should Know* by K. L. Kraemer and J. L. King for a discussion of the executive's role in planning and management.

[2]Further discussion of these findings can be found in Volume 2, Parts I and III, of this book. See also the EPRIS series reports available through NTIS, particularly *Information Functions, Services, and Administrative Policy* by Joseph R. Matthews, and in *Automation, Work, and Manpower Policy* by AnnaBelle Sartore and Kenneth L. Kraemer.

Analysis of Local Government Needs for Computer Technology

> The executive should insist on a thorough, accurate analysis of any ongoing
> government activity, including measures of its efficiency and productivity,
> before it is considered for automation or computer assistance.

Local government activities are fundamentally labor-intensive, and will
probably remain so in the future. Therefore, it is important to analyze any
potential advantages to using an automated system by looking at what changes
it will bring to the existing manual system. Some activities are greatly aug-
mented by automation, but others are not. Misapplications of technology can
be costly mistakes.

Government executives should have a clear understanding of how operations are performed without automation before the decision to automate is
made. With such an understanding it is possible to anticipate probable contributions of the automation, and to dispel arguments of potential benefits where
none are likely to emerge. Benchmark data on pre-automation performance
also allow for cost and performance comparison between the old system and
the new if the decision is made to automate.

Local governments should also look to the experiences of others with
comparable situations to see which functions are actually assisted by different
kinds of computer assistance. Experimenting with new applications is very
common among local governments, and it is usually possible to find another
government with similar characteristics and equipment that has tried a particular application before.

Top Management Support

> Top management support and involvement are essential to the success of a
> computerized information system.

All really successful local government computer systems have one thing
in common: they all enjoy full and dedicated support from top management,
including the chief executive and all major department heads. Computerized
information systems are major organizational undertakings, requiring substantial investment of money, time, and effort. Any effort to build and operate such
a system must have the firm support and backing of top management. Continued top management support is essential to survival of the system.

Management support entails more than just approval, as testified by the
number of systems that have started and failed on the basis of changing
approval status. Real management support requires commitment and involvement. Top management must be willing to work to obtain necessary funding
for the system, and must take an active role in seeing that the system is

properly run. In particular, chief executive participation is key in situations that cross departmental boundaries, while department heads are key to most application-related issues. But for any important situation, top management should take care when making decisions about the computer system.

Strategy and Control in System Building

A carefully developed strategy for change will assist in the process of system building.

Introduction of a computing system, or any major change in an existing system, represents an important organizational decision. The outcomes of that decision, good and bad, are largely affected by the way that change is implemented. Most organizations implement changes according to policies intended to pilot the change through from planning to final completion. Whether formal or informal, these policies represent a "strategy" used by management to bring about the change with as little trouble as possible.

The key to a successful strategy for change is in anticipating the likely outcomes of a change, and in planning ways to deal with them. To anticipate these outcomes requires a careful conception of what the post-change situation will be like, and an understanding of the required actions to reach that situation. Different systems and changes in systems bring different results, so a varied range of control mechanisms is useful. In general, there are three major kinds of development projects: automation of current information handling procedures, such as payroll processing or financial accounting; generalized software development for data handling, such as operating systems, teleprocessing systems, file management systems, and data management systems; and advanced applications that extend the scope of computer capabilities beyond straightforward processing to include complex search and retrieval, modeling, and computation. Often, advanced applications also involve large scale integration of data, data processing functions, and data flows as in such integrated systems as property files or criminal justice files.

Research indicates that for projects to automate simple procedures, the best control mechanisms are traditional cost and time schedules. However, for more complex development projects these traditional controls are less effective due to problems of cost overruns and slipping schedules. Such cases require development of more accurate scheduling and cost projections, and institution of periodic evaluation points for monitoring progress.

Procurement of Computing Capability

The decision of how to obtain computing capability is extremely important, and must be made on the basis of sound, comprehensive evaluation of alternatives.

The decision of how to obtain computing capability determines much of what will happen in the organization's information management efforts. All the available procurement alternatives entail substantial cost, but some can be much more effective than others for certain tasks. The procurement decision must be made with the direct and full involvement of the local government top management.

There are two main factors in the decision: whose equipment to use and who is to manage the operations. The four alternatives available to the local government are presented in Figure 8.

There are no clear-cut advantages to any of these alternatives that apply to all local governments. Organizational ownership and management is the most common arrangement, particularly in larger local governments, but this has been challenged recently in a few places by use of facility management agreements where local government computers are operated by an outside company. Also, many cities and counties have had success with buying services from a common source, and in joining together in consortiums to share facilities and management. These show particular promise for smaller jurisdictions.

Local government executives should insist on careful exploration of all reasonable alternatives for procurement before proceeding, and should contact those local governments with experience in the various approaches. In addition, loc mind the growing use of minicomputers that provide considerable computing capability at low cost. Minicomputers may be a viable alternative to large systems for some local governments.

Computer Impacts on the Organization

Introduction of computing technology has a substantial impact on the organization, as do major changes in the system after introduction. These impacts must be anticipated if they are to be dealt with effectively.

The decision to adopt computing technology is an important step for any organization. Likewise, any substantial changes in system have significant organizational impact. Many aspects of computing focus on such issues as manpower and personnel issues, or on the technology itself, but the overall planning and management aspect of computer impacts is broader. It is a perspective that encompasses all the other issues. Since use of computing technology in an organization entails interaction of social and technical systems, both kinds of systems must be understood before effective control is possible.

There are four elements of impacts that managers must understand. The first is the technical element involving the computer system and its performance as discussed in Chapter 7 of this volume. The second is the personnel element as discussed in Chapter 6. The third is the financial aspect of systems

FIGURE 8

Alternative Arrangements for Ownership and Management of Equipment

Management of the Facilities	Owned by the Local Government	Owned by an Outside Organization
Managed by the Local Government	*Owned and managed by the local government* Most larger local governments use this arrangement, and many smaller governments are adopting it with the advent of less expensive computing hardware. *Advantages:* Full government control of the equipment and its use, as well as potentials for economies of scale. *Disadvantages:* High investment and maintenance costs, even if the system is underused.	*Rental or Lease Arrangements* Some local governments use this arrangement, but it is more common in business situations. *Advantages:* Low investment costs, and relative ease in changing the system. *Disadvantages:* Less government control over system, and usually much higher overall equipment cost in long run.
Managed by an Outside Organization	*Facility Management* A few local governments have adopted this approach, among them, Orange County, Ca., San Bernardino, Ca., Colorado Springs, Colo., and Grand Rapids, Mich. *Advantages:* Government control over the system, frequently lower operating costs, removal of need for government management. *Disadvantage:* Less government control over management activities, absolute need for a good contract, and problems of changeover if converting from a government-managed situation.	*Service Bureaus and Regional Facilities* Many smaller local governments use service bureaus, and in effect buy service. Some small and medium-sized local governments have formed regional facilities that they share in common. These facilities include the Lane County, Oregon, Regional Information System; the Cincinnati-Hamilton County System; and the Southern California Metropolitan Data System. *Advantages:* Flexible utility, easy to adapt to needs, less management for participating governments, and often lower costs. *Disadvantages:* Little control for individual governments; cost-sharing difficult to make equitable, may be unreliable, requires much cooperation.

Source: Compiled by the authors.

discussed in Chapter 5. The fourth is the social-political impact as discussed in Chapter 8. The admonishment here is to encourage the executive to keep abreast of all impacts on the government brought by technological change.

Location of Computing Services within the Organization

Location of computing services should be decided on the grounds of meeting the organization's need for information, and not simply out of convenience.

Most local governments have initially located computing services in the finance department. This is natural, since most of the initial applications of computing have been financially oriented. If the finance department is and will remain the primary user, this arrangement is appropriate. This practice can have some drawbacks, however. By committing the computing resource to the finance department, the use and further development of the technology by other local government departments may be stifled. Non-finance department users might have difficulty gaining access to the computer resource because they have no control over it. In addition, because financial applications tend to be routine "housekeeping" operations (see Chapter 2), finance department control over the computer may retard development of more sophisticated uses of the technology that other departments might wish to implement.

If control of the technology by the finance department inhibits further use and development of the technology within the local government, it may be advisable to move the computing service into a separate, independent governmental department. This does not imply that a separate EDP department is necessarily a good thing. It means that organizational location of the computing service should be evaluated periodically to see if organizational needs are being met through existing arrangements.

The EDP Department

The process of developing and fully utilizing computer capability in larger local governments usually results in formation of a separate EDP department.

In larger cities (above 50,000 population), as new applications for various governmental activities are developed and put into use, an independent EDP department is often formed. This applies primarily to those organizations with centralized computing capability (see below). This helps to expedite management and control of the computing resource throughout the organization, and allows for easier access by different departments. This does not mean that all computer-related activity necessarily be centered in the EDP department, even if there is a centralized computer facility. It simply means there should be a centralized, independent authority to coordinate computing activity and to insure that needs of all users are met.

The EDP Manager

> The choice of an EDP Manager is very important, and must take into consideration an applicant's technical skills, management abilities, and understanding of local government.

While it is essential that an EDP manager have adequate technical skill, it is also important that he or she be a competent manager with an understanding of local government. The job of the EDP manager usually involves more leadership and administration than anything else. An effective EDP manager will most likely have frequent interaction with other managers in the local government. Without sound administrative ability, the EDP manager will find it difficult to run the EDP department or activity efficiently or effectively.

An understanding of local government is needed since the EDP department must serve the needs of other departments, local government managers, and elected officials. Local government is big business, but it is not the same as industry. Local governments perform a wider variety of functions than most businesses, they utilize a different personnel structure in most cases (civil service), and above all, they are governed by some distinctly political mechanism such as the mayor, city council, or board of supervisors. These characteristics of local government have a definite impact on the EDP manager's role and job. The EDP manager must be sensitive to the special needs of various department heads, political leaders, top local government, and even to citizens in some cases.

Centralization vs. Decentralization of Computing

> Centralization vs. decentralization of computing is a complex problem. Ultimately, the decision to centralize or decentralize computing must be made according to the kind of computing the organization does, the organizational structure of the government, and the management style of the governmental management.

The question of centralization vs. decentralization of computing is more complex than it first appears. It involves three elements: the computing facility itself, the analysts and programmers who service users, and the authority for computing in the organization. There is no research to clearly support centralization or decentralization of any of these elements of computing, but a great deal of literature has been written to support all points of view. Most of this literature focuses only on the issue of centralizing or decentralizing computer facilities. In general, the arguments in support of centralization cite better top management control, cost savings due to economies of scale, and efficiency from consolidation of personnel and hardware resources. Proponents of decentralization claim better service to users, greater flexibility in use of the technology, and costs that are about the same as centralized computing.

It is difficult to decide which of the arguments to believe; depending on the circumstances, they are both correct. Although the literature is not conclusive, there are several recommendations that can be made about centralizing or decentralizing particular elements of computing. The argument in support of centralized computing facilities is based on the claim that computing hardware is so expensive that it should be consolidated to achieve economies of scale. This used to be true, but the technology is changing rapidly. With the drastic decreases in the cost of computing hardware and the introduction of minicomputers, it is becoming reasonable to decentralize computing facilities, and even to consider use of "distributed computing" (see Chapter 7). Decentralized computer systems are being used by some local governments, such as Asheville-Buncome County, North Carolina, New York City, Los Angeles County, and Boston. It is possible that further decreases in hardware costs and new advances in technology, such as networking and telecommunications, will bring about a trend toward decentralization of computer facilities.

There is some evidence to support the claim that users receive better service if analysts and programmers are decentralized. In particular, users tend to be more satisfied when they have some direct control over the analysts and programmers who work on their applications. This can be accomplished by temporarily or permanently assigning EDP department staff members to user departments, or by actually requiring user departments to hire their own analysts and programmers. The latter alternative necessitates coordinating the hiring with the EDP department, and the EDP department itself must maintain programmers and analysts for system-level and special programming jobs. It should be noted that there are some exceptions to the advantages of decentralization of analysts and programmers. It may be appropriate to centralize all staff when the EDP shop is very small and cannot justify dedication of personnel to individual departments, or when the EDP department is organized around a data base management system (see Chapter 7) that requires close EDP department control over all system and data base activities. Even under data base management though, it might be advantageous to place several programmers and analysts at the service of departments to assist them in using the system.

There is strong evidence that centralization of authority for EDP is beneficial. Even if the government has numerous installations, it will probably be worthwhile to centralize authority for hardware purchases (possibly excluding purchase of small peripherals such as terminals), development priorities, large-scale software decisions (e.g., operating and teleprocessing systems), and data standards.

It is advisable to try to match the decision for centralization or decentralization with the organization's management philosophy. If the organization itself is highly centralized around an established and effective authority, a centralized approach will probably be effective. If the organization is highly decentralized, with substantial operating and management autonomy among departments, a decentralized system may be best. Any centralization-decentralization decision should take these factors into account.

Participants in Planning, Development, and Operation

It is important that all relevant parties participate in planning, development, and operation of computerized information systems.

In any local government there are individuals and groups who will be affected by a computerized information system. In order to insure ease of implementation and service to user needs, these people should be involved in planning, development, and operation activities related to the system. A mechanism to accomplish such participation is to establish policy boards for various issues. These boards can be made up of a mix of those affected by the system as related to a particular issue. The boards should include, where appropriate, elected officials, management, users, citizens, and data processing personnel. Examples of such boards already in operation in some local governments are privacy review boards, data security boards, user boards, computer acquisition and procurement boards, and information services policy boards.

Current research does not discuss the effectiveness of policy boards in given situations, nor is there clear and reliable evaluation of the impact of existing boards on actual policies and their implementation. Nevertheless, use of policy boards by local governments is increasing, and this can be regarded as a sensible effort to involve in the planning and policymaking process those who will be affected by a computerized information system.

Data Accuracy and Utility

Data accuracy is crucial to utility of any information system. Management should make every effort to insure that data in its computerized systems are accurate.

Regardless of how elaborate and sophisticated a computerized system is, it is useless if it contains inaccurate data. Inaccurate data can cause costly mistakes in operational application, can give rise to poor decisions based on poor information, and in the case of sensitive data on individuals, can cause considerable harm to citizens. Inaccuracies are usually generated in data collection, in coding, and in data input. They are almost always the result of human error or carelessness. It is up to the executive to insist on development and attainment of reasonable accuracy standards for the organization, and to insure cooperation among departments to see that these standards are met.

Security Concerns for Management

Local governments should take precautions to insure security of both their data and their computing installations.

Security is an important but often neglected need. Poor security can result in serious problems for management and for the whole local government operation. There are two major security issues: security of data, and security of computing facilities.

Security precautions for data must be taken to insure against accidental or intentional destruction or modification of data, and to prevent unauthorized access to data. The concerns here are both financial and legal. Destruction or improper modification of a data file can cost a substantial amount of money to correct. Unauthorized access to data or programs can lead to embezzlement, fraud, and misuse of local government services, as well as serious abuses of personal information (e.g., police records) for which the government is responsible. Data security can be attained by several means, ranging from simply not storing certain data on the system, to elaborate hardware and software protection systems. These might require technical expertise to implement, but the task of insisting on and insuring data security belongs to management.

Security of the installations mainly protects against accidental or intentional computer system damage or destruction. The need for such security should be obvious given the value of expensive computing equipment and facilities, but this need is frequently overlooked. The executive should request a complete security evaluation of the local government computing installation(s). This evaluation should assess threats from and recommend precautions against fire, flood, and other natural disasters, and from deliberate destructive acts by individuals. Following this evaluation, steps should be taken to bring security up to an acceptable level.

The Need for Evaluation

Frequent and thorough evaluations of computerized information systems should be conducted to insure a high level of efficiency and performance.

There are two purposes for frequent evaluation of computerized information systems: to see if the systems are meeting the design standards they were built to achieve, and to assess the design standards to see if they still conform to organizational needs. Given the high financial and personnel cost for developing and maintaining a computerized information system, evaluation must also relate costs to accomplishments of the system.

There are three kinds of evaluation that should take place: technical performance evaluation, financial evaluation, and policy evaluation. Monitoring and evaluating mechanisms for technical performance should be "built in" to the system to provide data on ongoing operations. Analysis of such data should be a continuous process. Periodically, it is advisable to bring in an outside auditing agent to assess the system and catch any problems that slip by in-house staff. Policies and procedures should be reviewed by management at regular intervals. Finally, a complete evaluation report should be prepared on an annual basis (or whenever appropriate), and distributed to all concerned parties. This should include proposals of steps to remedy existing problems, and a plan for implementing these remedies.

Summary

Planning and management are two of the most important aspects of any computerized information system undertaking. Computer systems bring substantial financial, personnel, and organizational impacts that can and should be anticipated and planned for. If managers take care to deal with likely problems before they arise, and are quick to act on problems that do arise, they will substantially increase the chances for success in their organizations' systems.

This chapter has covered a number of key issues in planning and management for computerized information systems. They can be summarized in the following points:

1. Planning is the first step in any computerized information system endeavor, and must be carried out with attention to all reasonable alternatives.

2. Top management involvement is essential to success of the system. Managers should be versed in all major issues of the system and its operation.

3. Changes in the organization will accompany the introduction and use of these systems, and the manager must anticipate and plan for these changes so the objectives of the organization will be achieved.

4. Evaluation of the computerized system should be required by top management to allow for proper review of current efforts, and to facilitate decision making about proposed new developments.

5

**FINANCIAL
CONSIDERATIONS**

Computers and computer-based information systems are very costly. It has been estimated that local governments alone spend over $1 billion per year on computing in the United States. Federal aid to state and local governments for computer-based systems is estimated at over $200 million annually. Local governments currently spend a little over 1 percent of their operating budgets on computing, and this figure is expected to reach 2-3 percent in the next decade.

Each local government periodically faces decisions on major expenditures for computerized systems. These decisions include purchase or rental of a computer, software purchases, software deployment, peripheral purchases, upgrading a current system, cost recovery strategies, and so on. This chapter provides basic guidance for dealing with financial considerations in computerized systems.[3]

Investment Strategies and Financial Evaluation

Local government managers should look upon commitment to computing as an investment decision, requiring careful evaluation of alternatives and risks as well as possible benefits.

The decision to acquire a computing capability entails future costs far beyond the initial computer procurement decision. Substantial future commit-

---

[3]Detailed discussion of the issues presented here can be found in Volume 2, Part II, of this book. See also the EPRIS project reprt, *Financial Aspects of Urban Information Systems* by Edward Schrems and George Duggar, available from the National Technical Information Service.

ments of funds for operating expenses, software, upgrading, and added personnel, are part of the computer "package" for most organizations. Local government executives should therefore treat any major decision regarding computing as an investment decision. The executive should ask what the system will really do, and at what price.

The best way to approach such investment decisions is with an investment strategy. This entails evaluating the potential benefits and costs of any proposed change, planning for ways to most effectively finance the change, and arranging for the most efficient way to bring the change about. Although an investment strategy will not insure optimal decisions, it will help insure more complete analysis of available alternatives if it is carefully developed.

Cost-Benefit Analysis

> Local government managers should consider using cost-benefit analysis as a method of evaluating computerized systems, but must recognize serious problems and limitations in its use.

Experts in the literature agree that cost-benefit analysis is an appropriate analytic tool for evaluation of existing or proposed computerized information systems. Cost-benefit analysis, in general terms, is a procedure for aggregating costs of an information system and comparing that aggregate cost with some measure of benefits derived from the system's use. There are a few examples of cost-benefit analyses performed on local government computerized systems, such as one done for the Regional Information Systems in the Lane County, Oregon, system. These examples are described in greater detail in Volume 2, Part II, of this book, and critical review of these examples is recommended.

The best time to perform cost-benefit analysis is prior to automation as an aid to determining whether a project should be undertaken. The extent of the analysis may vary, depending upon the size of the planned investment. Likewise, the analysis may take different forms, varying from systematic collection of benefits and costs of comparable systems, to a formal analysis of the planned project.

If cost-benefit analysis is done, some kind of audit should be performed after the system is implemented to determine whether anticipated benefits are being realized, and whether estimated costs prove correct. This will not only aid future analysis by providing better basis for estimates, but also will increase the confidence of policymakers in the results of analysis, even when the estimates prove to be inaccurate in any one case.

Despite the value of cost-benefit analysis, the utility of the technique is constrained by four serious considerations that should be mentioned. First, the analysis is difficult. There are no simple procedures or formulae for precisely determining costs or benefits from an information system. Errors of double-counting, oversight, and hidden costs make even the best of analyses somewhat loose. The examples of analyses in the literature do not provide comprehensive guidance of high quality. Any government undertaking a cost-benefit analysis on its information system should understand that the technique demands a strong commitment of staff resources to do the analysis if it is to be useful.

Second, any reasonable cost-benefit analysis requires use of a "discount rate" to apply to future costs and benefits.[4] Unfortunately, there is widespread disagreement about appropriate discount rates for all public expenditures, including expenditures for computing. Because of this confusion, many local governments simply do not use a discounting factor. This can seriously damage the validity of a cost-benefit analysis, since it assumes that the future utilities of all alternative uses of the local government's resources are equal--an obvious error. Despite the problems with setting a discount rate for an expenditure, it is essential that a rational attempt be made. A helpful discussion of discount rate determination can be found in Volume 2, Part II, of this book.

The third limitation in cost-benefit analysis is the fact that many local governments, particularly smaller ones, lack analysts with the expertise required to perform a complete analysis. People with such expertise are relatively rare in local government, but may be available in larger governments. If there is no one available with sufficient skill to perform a cost-benefit analysis, it should not be undertaken. Some local governments have made use of consultants from business and universities to perform their analyses for them. This can be a solution, provided the consultant has both professional expertise and an insight into the workings of the particular local government.

The fourth consideration is the possibility that any advantage gained from performing a rigorous cost-benefit analysis might not justify performing that analysis. Due to the difficulties mentioned above, cost-benefit analysis can itself be costly in excess of the benefits it produces. This problem can be alleviated somewhat by performing analysis in steps. Begin with study of cost-benefit analyses conducted on similar circumstances in other local governments, then proceed with evaluation of simple, quantifiable costs and cost savings in your local government situation. If this proves worthwhile, the analysis can proceed to evaluation of more difficult items.

These limitations should not be taken as reasons to avoid cost-benefit analysis. Rather, they provide guidance on some of the difficulties in performing an effective, useful analysis that will meet the local government's needs.

---

[4]A "discount rate" is used to calculate which alternative investment offers the greatest dollar payoff over time. The easiest way to understand this is to think of whether it is better to receive a dollar today or a dollar one year from now. Obviously, it is better to receive the dollar today because it can earn interest for a year, and thereby be worth more than a dollar a year from now. The discount rate in this case is equal to the interest rate on the dollar being saved.

Financing a Data Processing Activity

Six alternatives for financing data processing activity should be evaluated before a financing method is chosen.

There are six methods of financing a data processing activity: loans, bond issues, special tax levies, grants, federal revenue sharing, and budget line item. Most computer systems are financed through the operating budget, or through grants from federal or other agencies.

Each method has inherent costs and advantages that must be considered. For example, loans have a higher interest than do bonds, but they do not require voter approval as do bond issues. In addition, there are legal constraints on certain kinds of financing methods available to local governments, varying from state to state and government to government. It is important when considering financing methods to assess the future availability of funds. This is especially true with external funding from the federal government or other agencies. In most cases the external funding helps in development phases, but is withdrawn eventually, leaving the full financial burden of the system on the local government.

There is, unfortunately, insufficient systematic research literature comparing various financing methods to determine any method as clearly better. This depends on the conditions at the local level to a large extent, so what works well for one local government may not work for another. Careful analysis of alternatives must take place at the local government, with a decision based on local conditions.

Acquiring Computing Capability

The choice of how to acquire a computer capability should encompass an evaluation of all reasonable methods, including sharing of facilities with another organization or government.

This subject was discussed in Chapter 4, but it will be considered here from a financial perspective. As shown in Chapter 4, there are basically four ways to acquire computing capability: full ownership and operation by the local government; joint ownership and control with others; acquiring service through a private vendor; and facility management. Use of these methods of acquiring data processing capability tends to vary with local government size. Large cities and counties almost always own and operate their own computing facilities, while smaller jurisdictions tend to use external procurement methods such as timesharing or service bureaus.

Ownership seems to require a population of about 50,000 or more before it becomes economically justifiable based on demands and costs. Of course, as mentioned, the cost of hardware is going down while the cost of software is going up, and this may change the above rule of thumb. Local government executives should compare their local jurisdictions with others of comparable size to determine trends. Also, computer equipment can be brought on-site by means other than straight purchase, such as rental or lease (see below).

Joint ownership offers two financial advantages to smaller local governments: it tends to reduce the cost for hardware per participant, and it tends to reduce the cost of maintenance and software. This approach offers a chance to capitalize on "economies of scale" from a larger operation than any government could afford on its own. Of course, this kind of joint arrangement can increase other costs, such as the costs of communication and negotiation involved in multiple ownership.

Acquiring service from a private vendor, such as a service bureau or a local bank, is much like any other contract service. The local government must expect to pay a portion of the vendor's overhead and profit as reflected in the charges for service, and the local government may have little say in the kinds of service the vendor provides. This arrangement seems to be most sensible for those cases where a small local government wants a few routine applications such as payroll processing done periodically.

Facilities management, a relative newcomer to the list of procurement alternatives, offers a chance to firmly fix costs for operation for a period of five years or longer, depending on the contract used. Because the process is new and little study has been made, it is not clear whether the local government saves any money by using facilities management as opposed to outright ownership. The contractual nature of facilities management may tend to discourage expansion of data processing use by the government, yet because the facilities management contractor makes more money if the system is expanded, an accommodation can be reached. At any rate, so few local governments are using this approach it is difficult to know the real financial payoffs it offers.

Rent, Lease, or Buy?

> Research does not show any clear advantage to renting, leasing, or buying computer equipment, so each local government must analyze its own situation with care and in light of experiences of others.

If a local government decides to procure its own computer capability, it has three options: rent the equipment, lease it, or buy it. The only substantial literature on these alternatives deals with the experiences of business and the federal government. In general, both business and the federal government find it advantageous to buy their computer equipment. However, local governments lack the tax benefits of business and the capabilities for internal transfer or resale of equipment of the federal government, so such experience has little comparability to local governments.

In a nutshell, each method offers an exchange of money for the flexibility to change computing equipment in the short run. Rentals offer maximum flexibility but a higher price. Leasing costs less, but usually entails minimum-time lease agreements. Purchase costs the least in the long run, but offers flexibility. It should be noted, however, that flexibility is more of an ideal than a reality for most information system installations, regardless of how their equipment is acquired. The proponents of system flexibility often imply that one computer can be moved out and another moved in with relative ease under a lease or rent option. This argument belies the true cost of such a change. It is not economical in the vast majority of situations to frequently change vendors, or even to change systems from the same vendor, due to the cost of transferring applications and data files, and retraining personnel. A computer procurement option that offers high flexibility in changing computer systems may have an advantage in some situations, such as meeting a short-term need, but these are exceptions. Given this situation, each local government should carefully consider its own situation in light of the options available, and should seek the advice of other governments of comparable size and operation that have had experience with the different alternatives.

Controlling the Computing Resource

> Local governments should manage computing capabilities and data as resources to be allocated where need is greatest and benefit highest, given each government's state of development.

Computing capabilities and data bases are local goverment resources, just as are automobiles, typewriters, and office space. They must be managed as resources if their use is to result in maximum benefit at least cost to the local government. This means these resources must go to meet those needs that offer the highest benefit when met.

According to economic research, resource management for information systems is most effectively provided through pricing and accounting mechanisms (to be discussed below). These mechanisms serve to bring greater efficiency in use of the resource, recovery of costs of the resource, and better determination of priority for use. It is the responsibility of the local government executive to oversee proper control of computer and data resources. Proper control may require using incentives to expand use of data processing, as when the government is first beginning to use computers, or it may require mechanisms to restrict use when demand for data processing exceeds capacity. This will depend on the local government's state of development in using EDP, and on the kinds of uses made of it. In any case, this overall responsibility should not be permanently delegated to any one department for reasons discussed in Chapter 4 of this volume.

Allocating Computer Resources

> When computing and data resources must be shared among several users or departments, an economic allocation scheme should be applied to insure use in line with management goals.

Computing and data resources, like most resources, are under different demands at different times. As mentioned above, there are times when use should be encouraged; other times when use should be discouraged. In order to match user demands for the resource to capacity of the resource, there must either be (1) a big enough information system to handle any demand at any time, (2) a mechanism for spreading demand for a smaller system among the users, or (3) some means of increasing use in the case of slack capacity. Because information systems are expensive resources and local governments desire to have their resources productively employed, allocation schemes are a necessity if demand is to be matched to supply over many users or departments.

Allocation schemes primarily control for three problems: extent of use, priority of use, and cost recovery. Extent of use refers to increasing or decreasing aggregate demand on the system. When potential use exceeds capacity of the system, the supply of computing resource must be directed to users in a way to obtain maximum benefit. This may entail establishment of maximum allowance of computer time to some departments. When capacity exceeds demand, some way of encouraging users to use the system is needed. Priority of use means establishing which jobs shall be processed first when there is high demand. Cost recovery allocation is necessary if the local government does not "give away" computing resources to departments as a free good.

If the system is under-utilized and there is a sensible reason to encourage use (such as to familiarize people with computing), there are several incentives to accomplish this: the executive can insist that certain reporting activities take place using computing; programmers and analysts can be assigned to departments to work at implementing applications; and computing service can be given away to departments as a free good. These incentives will work, depending on local circumstances.

If demand exceeds supply, there are three basic schemes for allocation (aside from simply meeting demand by getting more computing capacity). First is to determine each case on its merits, then allocate by administrative decision. Second is to establish a policy that allocates the resource based on some criteria: a strategy much less demanding of administrative resources. Third is to charge a price for use of the resource. The first two are basically administrative decisions imposed on users from above; the third is an economic mechanism. All three allocation schemes can be used in a mix if necessary, depending on the needs of the situation.

Charging for Computer Resources

Charging users for computer resources is considered an excellent allocation method, particularly if charges are in "hard" money.

Research indicates that charging for computer resources is an effective allocation technique. Charging a price for resources is a way of solving the three allocation problems mentioned above. Charges can be raised or lowered to increase or decrease demand; they can be set higher during peak demand periods to establish job priority; and they can be used as a cost recovery mechanism. Charging for use is the only scheme that can solve all three problems simultaneously.

Evidence suggests that charging users "hard" money for computing will produce more efficient allocation than charging "soft" money. "Hard" money is money that can be used to purchase anything the department desires in doing its job. "Soft" money, on the other hand, is earmarked for a particular purchase such as computing. Soft money is not really considered a resource to departments in the same way hard money is, so soft money is usually used less carefully by the departments. Of course, this assumes that the executive wants to maximize efficiency of use. This may not be the case in situations where there is excess capacity, and incentives are needed to increase use.

There is one serious problem in developing an effective charging scheme: setting a proper price. There are three alternatives (profit maximizing pricing, average cost pricing, and marginal cost pricing) discussed in the literature, but no consensus exists as to which is best for a local government computing environment. See Volume 2, Part II, for a discussion of these pricing methods.

Accounting Practices for Data Processing Activities

If users are charged for computing use, an effective mechanism to account for use of computer resources can probably be obtained from available packaged software, provided that the mechanism meets the minimmum requirements listed below.

Any mechanism or plan used to account for computing resources should contain six characteristics:

1. *Reproducibility*. Charges should be independent of system conditions at any time, i.e., when the job runs or what other jobs run with it.
2. *Equitability*. Jobs requiring more resources should pay more.

3. *Cost Recovery*. The scheme should permit cost recovery. Even though economists dispute the need for this criterion, organizational considerations may require it.

4. *Auditability*. There should be provisions for auditing charges.

5. *Encouragement of Efficiency Hardware Use*. The mechanism should be built to foster the most efficiency, least-cost use of hardware.

6. *Allowance for Cost Estimation*. The mechanism should enable users to estimate probable costs for jobs and cost differences from program changes.

Since there is no research that systematically compares and evaluates specific software packages or accounting mechanisms, it is necessary for each local government to assess the utility of available packages according to the above criteria and its own special needs.

Financial Evaluation of Performance

Financial evaluation of a computer system should be undertaken to provide for budgetary review, assessment of current costs and benefits, and forecasting the future financial needs of the system.

Financial evaluation of a computer system includes accounting and budgetary review, cost benefit analysis, and forecasting. Accounting and budgetary review is necessary to insure that the system activity is meeting budgetary requirements, and that funding levels are adequate for achieving expected performance levels. Cost-benefit analysis, discussed earlier, can be an ongoing process that should be integrated into the overall system evaluation effort. Forecasting entails using current financial, budgetary, and cost-benefit information to predict the future needs of the information for planning purposes. By viewing all three of these activities as part of overall evaluation activity, the system can be brought under closer and more precise financial control.

Summary

As mentioned at the beginning of this chapter, local government top management should bear the responsibility for maintaining financial control over its computerized information systems. This can be accomplished through thoughtful handling of four key financial aspects of computerized systems.

1. Evaluation, including cost-benefit analysis, budgetary review, forecasting, and accounting procedures.

2. Financing, including analysis of all available alternatives for covering the costs of data processing.

3. Procurement, including careful analysis of different sources of computing capability to make use of the most beneficial supply package available.

4. Control, including allocation mechanisms and charging schemes to make most efficient use of scarce computing resources.

CHAPTER

6

MANPOWER
CONCERNS AND
PERSONNEL
POLICY

Regardless of the capabilities that computer systems offer to local governments, they can only be realized if local government personnel are willing and able to use the systems. Computing technology, like any other major technology, has an impact on the organizations that adopt it. This means that an introduction of automation will probably bring significant changes in the way employees behave, interact with one another, and perform their tasks. Some of these changes are positive; others negative. Positive changes can be welcomed as genuine benefits from use of the computer. But negative changes must be dealt with thoughtfully if the local government wishes to avoid personnel problems.[5]

Computers and Personnel Costs

Use of computing and automation frequently does not result in reduced overall personnel costs.

A common argument in support of computer use is that it will reduce overall personnel costs. In general, this is not true. Most organizations replace some lower-paid clerical staff with fewer but higher-paid professional and EDP staff, so overall salary expenses tend to remain about equal. In addition, many

---

[5]The following recommendations and findings are discussed in greater detail in Volume 2, Part III, of this book, and in the EPRIS project report, *Automation, Work, and Manpower Policy* by AnnaBelle Sartore and Kenneth L. Kraemer, available from the National Technical Information Service.

organizations maintain the older manual systems as back-up, requiring a number of clerical personnel not really needed by the new EDP operation.

Introduction of computing does frequently "save" personnel costs when the computer increases an organization's capability to perform some critical tasks without a proportional increase in labor cost for those tasks. Most often, this occurs when a government's need for data processing is expanding rapidly, such as in areas where there is a high rate of population growth. If a community's population is increasing slowly, it's less likely that a great personnel saving will be realized from automation of information processing. In these cases, the cost "saving" can result from being able to do more tasks with the same personnel expenditure, rather than the same task with fewer expenditures. Management should carefully question claims that computerization of tasks will save the organization large amounts of money in personnel cost. The experiences of other organizations generally do not bear this out.

Computer Impacts on People and Their Attitudes

Computing technology impacts people directly by forcing changes in procedures and habits, and indirectly by requiring them to learn new skills and adopt new communication patterns. These impacts often result in personnel problems which must be anticipated and dealt with carefully.

People's adjustment to technological change depends on their background, education, and previous experience with the technology or with similar organizational change. When the presence of computing technology results in changes in habits, procedures, and communication patterns within organizations, employees are often confused and frustrated about their roles and jobs. They may perceive that they are losing influence relative to others, or that the security of their job is threatened. Such worries and problems are natural, and may result in no harm to the employee or to organizational performance. But they can result in employee dissatisfaction and reduced productivity--a situation detrimental to both the person and the organization.

It is important that managers be sensitive to the way employees interact with the organization before a major change is introduced. This way they can spot likely problems to result from the change. Attitudes toward a new technology frequently evolve in stages from hostility, to apathy, to acceptance. A clear understanding of employee attitudes and needs prior to the technological change will assist this adaptation process and smooth over rough spots after the change.

Personnel from different functional areas and levels tend to respond to changes brought by computing in different ways. Upper management employees often object to a perceived loss of power and control when computing is introduced, and when any major conversion to automation takes place.

Middle managers tend to be sensitive to perceived routinization of their jobs, and a new "subservience" to demands of the technology. Also, computing can add new data-related chores to their jobs, making their work more difficult. If management does not respond and adapt to the technology with supportive policies, then attitudes of top and middle management will retard adaptation by the rest of the organization. A strong management aversion to technological change like computing may be a good reason for the organization to make do with traditional methods.

Supervisory and clerical personnel most often object to imposition of a rigid routine that de-personalizes their jobs and robs them of intrinsic work rewards, such as praise for creativity and a chance to excel as individual performers. In addition, computing technology often brings an intensified performance-monitoring capability based on error rates and speed. Clerical personnel sometimes feel this enhances a supervisor's ability to "control" them: a belief that can cause friction between employees at different levels. If a job's intrinsic rewards are decreased by the technological change, employees should be compensated in other ways.

EDP personnel frequently have difficulties communicating with individuals in the rest of the organization, particularly user departments. They are often viewed as elitists who support the data processing profession at the expense of the organization. Moreover, they are often paid more than individuals in other departments with more seniority. These communication problems can best be dealt with by insuring that data processing and user personnel work together to meet user needs, and by policies that avoid giving technological personnel preferential treatment.

Computers and Job Displacement

It is advisable whenever possible to deal with people whose jobs have been displaced by computing by transfer within the organization, or by retraining and placement in EDP-related jobs, rather than by simple dismissal.

Alternatives to simple dismissal of displaced employees have worked well for several reasons. First, those jobs most directly affected by computerization (e.g., low level clerical and supervisory jobs) have traditionally had high turnover rates anyway, and normal attrition usually takes care of the problem. Second, the EDP function often creates needs for personnel with clerical-like skills, such as keypunching or data entry operators, that can be recruited and trained from displaced personnel. This has the advantage of offering internal job mobility to lower-level clerical personnel throughout the organization.

There has recently been a trend toward filling EDP-related jobs at all levels with people from within the organization. This has several advantages. It avoids external recruitment which necessitates offering highly competitive salaries. Also, since qualified technical labor is often in short supply, turnover is usually high among skilled externally hired EDP personnel. Finally, the internally recruited employee knows the organization and the organization knows the employee: a highly advantageous situation, since the employee is adjusted to the environment, and the organization already has a good notion of the employee's ability based on past performance. Of course, internal recruitment requires that the employee have sufficient aptitude to handle the new task, and that the organization have sufficient resources for needed retraining.

When dismissal of a large number of displaced personnel is necessary, it is in the organization's interest to publish the retention and dismissal policy as early as practical. This helps to alleviate employee fears, and to encourage those likely to be retained not to leave.

Computer Impacts on Job Tasks

> Job tasks in a computerized setting are integrally related to the way the system is designed and how it is used.

Changes in technology impact job tasks by adding, changing, or eliminating certain job activities. The majority of impacts occur closest to the computing technology itself, usually in the data processing department and in major user departments. In general, changes in job tasks are concentrated at lower job levels, such as clerical and data entry positions, and decrease as one moves toward management level positions.

Upper management personnel tend to see little direct impact on job tasks because they have less direct contact with the technology. This may change in the future as more management-oriented computer applications are developed and put into use. Many middle-management jobs now require some technical interaction, so impact on job task has been stronger here. The research indicates that the major problem middle managers face in computing is information extremes--inability to get proper information, or on the opposite extreme, information overload. Since a middle manager must report to top management by gathering and "filtering" information from various sources, it is critical that information be readily available. Changes in the system can result in delays that make it difficult for a middle manager to perform this task or, conversely, can create added work for the middle manager by providing redundant information that requires substantially more "filtering."

Supervisory and clerical personnel usually perform tasks that require adherence to rules and time schedules, and that rely on an understanding of the technical system. Job performance is usually paced, and is evaluated on accuracy and precision. Output is measured for speed and error rates traceable directly to individual employees. Computerization tends to increase routine and decrease flexibility in individual task performance. If employees are comfortable with the technology, increased productivity can result. If employees are uncomfortable and unhappy in their jobs, productivity can decline through slowdowns, increased error rates, and increased turnover. Employees should be selected to match the realities of the work environment.

Computer personnel and technical personnel in user departments are most directly affected by changes in the technology since their jobs are dependent on the computer system and its design. Programmers and analysts who must implement changes on the computer system itself are often under considerable pressure due to needs and demands for change in the system or applications. This pressure can result in poorer productivity when the tasks placed on these personnel are not planned and scheduled by reasonable priorities. Management should remember that system design and programming are in many ways creative activities requiring insight and imagination as well as technical skills. Creative and imaginative people must be given adequate time to do their tasks if they are to perform well. Therefore, it is important that policies for system development and utilization recognize the special needs of technical personnel in order to realize maximum results for both the individuals and the organization.

One final point should be made about the relationship of the computerized information system to job tasks in service departments such as welfare and police. It is important that the system's impact on the scheduling and workload reporting not have a detrimental effect on the service being performed. This can happen if the reporting system uses an inappropriate measure of employee performance. For example, if a welfare caseworker is being evaluated on the basis of a workload reporting system that measures only the number of client contacts made per week, the caseworker may try to maximize contacts at the expense of the quality of each contact made. This can detract from the true purpose of the caseworker's job, and offer an inaccurate picture of caseworker performance. Many employees in service professions such as police and welfare resent the prospect that they may be evaluated by inappropriate measures that do not reflect their real job roles.

Employee Interaction with the Computer

Input and output characteristics of the computerized system drastically affect the system's utility to users, so it is important to choose a system with characteristics that help rather than hinder employee performance.

Data can be put into a computer in various ways: through cards, through magnetic tape, through terminals, or through paper tape. But originally, most data first have to be put on one of these media by a coding process requiring use of a keypunch, terminal, or teletype machine. Choice of data entry methods is important, and should be tailored to the kinds of data the system uses. This decision is primarily dependent on local circumstances, and the preferences of the data entry personnel should be taken into account.

The output from a computer can be summarized by an analyst or left relatively raw. Summarization tends to increase the speed and quality of decisions based on computer output, but reduces the user's confidence in such decisions. Raw data output tends to decrease both speed and quality of decisions, but increases the confidence of the user in each decision. Obviously, output format must be tailored to combined needs for actual quality and speed of decisions, and the confidence with which these decisions are made.

The choice of batch vs. interactive capability, in addition to technical and cost concerns, depends on the kind of processing task to be performed, the required turn-around time, and the availability of terminals. Batch processing generally results in slower turn-around time than interactive processing, but requires no terminals, less computer time, and less sophistication from users. Interactive processing is usually faster, and can offer great versatility to the user, but is more costly and complex. Employees with little training usually have a more difficult time making effective use of interactive systems.

Computers and Personnel Policies

It is advisable to have well-formulated personnel policies to facilitate introduction and use of computing technology.

Transition from non-computerized operations to computerized operations for any new application is a continuous process, lasting from one to five years. This transition period is both necessary and beneficial for the organization. The technology is meant to serve human needs, but people must adapt to its use. It is worthwhile to avoid disruption of the organization by giving employees a chance to adjust.

Once a system is established and operational, employee adjustment often is not yet complete. Computer technology is a rapidly evolving field, and most organizations are constantly trying to upgrade their systems and expand system use. This means the organization and its employees must constantly adapt to changes.

There are ten guidelines for personnel policies that will facilitate adaptation to the technology or any changes in the system.

1. Personnel policies should have an organizational focus, and should capitalize on available in-house personnel resources.

2. The policies should reflect the organization's management philosophy.

3. They should be used to coordinate computer-related jobs with non-computer-related jobs.

4. They should try to integrate the technology with the organizational environment.

5. They should be used to match the potential of the technology with needs of the employees.

6. They should be flexible.

7. They should be well coordinated, should be fully explained to employees, and whenever possible, should be introduced sequentially.

8. They should be adjusted as needed to correspond to changes in the technology.

9. They should allow for complaints about the technology.

10. They should reward acceptance and use of the technology.

These ten recommendations will help in creating personnel policies that assist introduction and subsequent use of the technology in the organization.

Recruiting EDP Personnel

Recruitment and selection of quality personnel is essential to success of an information system, but the recruiting and selection process is often faulty.

It is relatively easy to attract applicants to job openings in EDP, provided that salaries and benefits offered are comparable to the general market. Conversely, it is difficult to attract quality personnel if compensation is not competitive. This is frequently a major problem for governments outside large metropolitan areas where salaries of government employees are generally lower. It also is frequently a problem for governments when EDP is a division of another department, since salaries of that department's management personnel tend to set the upper limit on the salaries of EDP personnel. Although seldom discussed openly, the problem of competing pay scales for EDP personnel tends to be a factor in the push to give departmental status to EDP.

The major problem beyond competitive compensation in EDP personnel recruitment is the selection process. There are no highly reliable selection methods that serve as predictors of job performance. Education and experience are the most commonly used selection criteria, but both suffer from problems. With education there is a high variability in emphasis and quality between different institutions, making educational background a poor indicator of a person from a particular school being able to do the job that needs to be done. Prior experience, while somewhat more specific, is relevant only to the prospective employee's performance on the system and software previously used. There is no guarantee that the employee will be able to do as well on a new system or with different software. In addition, prior training may have been carried out with equipment and procedures made obsolete by technological advancements. Finally, there is no well developed, standard aptitude test for programmers and analysts.

The executive in charge of hiring EDP personnel should therefore use two approaches in recruiting and selection. First, some combination of the above criteria should be used. These can be weighted according to the amount of information available on each. For example, the employer may be very familiar with the operation where the prospective employee formerly worked. When using a combination, the criteria should be applied consistently to show which predictions of performance tend to be more reliable. Second, use of a probationary period for all new EDP employees will make it easier to evaluate job performance before making a full job commitment.

Training EDP Personnel

> It is advisable to have training capability for EDP personnel, both to train new personnel brought into the organization, and to update older personnel in new methods and techniques.

In the case of new EDP and computer-related employees, training is often required to introduce the details of the information system, and to integrate the new employees with existing staff. In general, training helps new employees to learn both technical and organizational procedures, and improves their attitude toward the system and the organization.

If the local government is large enough to warrant, this training can be supplied with in-house resources, and usually with excellent results. Large municipal governments are now turning to in-house training, and are often willing to assist smaller governments in training. Such cooperation reduces the major problem of maintaining a costly training staff and program, plus facilitates sharing of these ideas.

If the decision is made to go outside for training, there are three choices: manufacturers' schools, colleges and universities, and technical and business schools. Manufacturers' schools have traditionally provided most training for EDP personnel. Advantages of this approach are that manufacturers' schools know the equipment and software very well, and make an effort to meet the technical person's need for information. Disadvantages are that the training is often not related to the job the employee does, and is highly technical. Another, less recognized disadvantage to manufacturer training is that it can tend to get employees "locked-in" on use of only the systems made by that manufacturer. This can lead to bias toward a particular brand of equipment due simply to familiarity, even when another system is clearly the better choice.

Colleges and universities train a great many people in computer sciences, though sometimes this training is beyond the needs of the technician and may be concentrated on conceptual problems in computer science. This may be a good training ground for senior programmers and analysts, but probably goes beyond what is needed for normal staff training. While there is little research on the subject, this lack of intermediate training is probably being filled somewhat by growth of computer-related classes being taught in community (junior) colleges. These courses are often taught by practitioners, and have a very practical emphasis. A major advantage to community college training is that it tends to be inexpensive compared to larger colleges and universities. Once again, training is not generally job-related.

Technical schools and business colleges vary in both quality and emphasis of their instruction. The research is sparse about the effectiveness of such training, but overall, the use of these schools is not recommended because they are expensive, their course content is often dated, and instructional quality is questionable.

It is a good practice to check with other local governments about their experiences with training. Often they can provide valuable assistance on where to go for training services.

Training Other Personnel in EDP Uses

Training in relevant aspects of the computerized information system should be provided to any employees who are affected by the system.

A computerized information system is an organizational resource that should be understood by any people in the organization who are affected by it. In a small organization this usually means everyone, but even in larger organizations it is worthwhile to include as many employees as possible in training of this sort. This training should include an orientation to the system, with instruction on how the system relates to each job and employee. Beyond this rudimentary introduction, training should fit the level to which an employee uses, depends upon, or is impacted by the system.

Top managers in particular should be well-versed in the system, including its configuration, applications, and uses. Top managers should be trained in management techniques for efficient use of computer systems, and should be versed in the applications, potentials, and impacts of EDP. Many managers are now engaged in this kind of training through seminars and workshops offered by various professional associations.

Users and potential users should be trained in both technical and conceptual aspects of the system, particularly as related to their jobs. This is especially important if users are or soon will be interacting with the computer "on-line."

Promotion Policies and Career Ladders for EDP Personnel

Policies should be developed to provide EDP personnel career ladders both within the data processing department, and into other related departments.

As mentioned earlier, it is often advantageous to retain personnel displaced by a computerized system for EDP-related jobs. Likewise, promotion from within to fill vacant higher-level positions offers many advantages, provided the individual has the aptitude and the organization can afford training.

Promotion policy for EDP personnel is a bigger problem than that, however. EDP departments usually are plagued by high turnover of staff because computer-related personnel see little chance for promotion and reward within the government organization. High turnover is very destructive to quality and stability of computer services, and should be avoided if possible. This can be accomplished to a large extent by developing clear career paths for EDP personnel. These paths can take several directions: promotion within job classification, promotion across job classifications within the department, and promotions out of the EDP department into staff or management roles.

An example of a promotion within a classification would be from equipment operator, to computer operator, to chief console operator. This kind of promotion keeps highly skilled people in roles where they can exercise their skills, and can train others. Promotion across classifications is common, for example, from computer operator to programmer. This kind of promotion can be rewarding for the employee, particularly if salaries differ substantially across classifications. It is also logical to promote qualified people to jobs where they can do the most good, which usually means eventual re-classification. However, cross-classification promotions can have the effect of removing the most highly skilled people from classifications where they could be used for training and other important work.

Promotion out of the EDP department generally is less successful than other promotion practices. EDP personnel are often technically trained in skills irrelevant to non-EDP jobs, and may be unskilled in areas needed in the new department. In addition, technical EDP people often command salaries that make them noncompetitive with people in other departments. This does not imply that cross-departmental promotions cannot work out. They often do when the employee continues to perform a similar technical task such as analysis in the new department. But evidence suggests that most cross-departmental promotions are imperfect matches of talents with needs, both for the individual and the organization.

One alternative worth considering is retraining of technical EDP personnel with proper aptitudes to be "boundary spanners" between users, management, and data processing. Research indicates that individuals with such training are very useful to the organization. Another approach is to train employees from user departments to be technical EDP personnel. Although there is no research to show the effectiveness of this approach, several local governments are using it, and claim success.

Wages and Salaries of EDP Personnel

Wage and salary structures for EDP personnel should be dealt with carefully to provide sufficient recruiting attraction, while avoiding lopsided salaries between EDP and other departments.

Salaries for EDP personnel, on the average, are higher than salaries of comparable personnel in other departments. This is a function of high market demand and scarce supply of talented EDP personnel. Average salaries for computer-related personnel in many local governments, particularly larger governments, are the same or higher than salaries of comparable personnel in private industry.

These facts indicate need for three policies. First, benefits for non-EDP personnel should be stressed to make up for differences in salary between EDP and non-EDP personnel due to market conditions. The law of supply and demand dictates that scarce commodities like qualified EDP personnel will cost more, and the local government must pay the price for talent, but it may be wise to compensate non-EDP employees wherever possible for such differences in salary. Second, local government executives should periodically review prevailing salary levels for non-government EDP personnel to keep the local government's salary structure more in line with true market conditions. In addition, many municipalities offer more attractive fringe benefits than do private enterprises, and these should be stressed when recruiting EDP personnel. Third, the executive should review the organizational structure surrounding EDP, including the location of the EDP function in the organization, to insure that this structure facilitates proper handling of compensation, promotion, and all other aspects of EDP personnel.

Ethical Aspects of Personnel Policies

Managers should recognize that personnel policies can be used to unfairly manipulate and control personnel, often resulting in problems for both personnel and the organization.

The manager is in a position to direct and control the development and function of the organization through his policies. This authority is necessary if the manager is to be effective at carrying out the responsibilities he is faced with. However, this authority also places the manager in a position to unfairly coerce, control, and manipulate employees.

There are numerous detrimental effects of such abuse of management prerogative. Excessive harassment and manipulation of people is often damaging to productivity in the short run, and to overall organizational success in the long run. Most people do not like to be taken advantage of and learn soon enough when they are being manipulated for someone else's benefit. Individual employees can suffer from such treatment by developing insecurities about their job, dissatisfaction with their work, and animosity toward their superiors from whom they should be receiving direction and encouragement. The organization can suffer from loss of employee morale, slowdowns in productivity, and higher turnover rates. These effects can make the operation of an entire department unsatisfactory, and in the case of a central support department like data processing, can be very damaging to the local government.

But aside from potential detrimental effects from abuses of management control, there is the issue of ethical responsibility. It is a well documented fact that the attitudes and behavior of leaders filter down through their organizations, and eventually impact those that the organizations employ and serve. This places a responsibility on executives to be conscious of their behavior, and to ask themselves if they think their policies are fair as well as effective. This may require periodic review, in which the executive seeks honest feedback from subordinates.

Summary

This chapter reviewed key points about manpower concerns and personnel policy related to local government information systems. These key points can be summarized by four brief statements:

1. Qualified, willing personnel are essential to success of an information system.

2. Information technology has an impact on personnel habits, procedures, communications, and behavior. The effect of this impact may be either good or bad, depending on how the technology is introduced and managed.

3. The managers of the local government can, to a large extent, control the effects of information technology on employees through use of well planned, carefully implemented personnel policies.

4. The managers have a responsibility to see that their policies are not only effective, but are fair to local government personnel as well.

7

Computing technology is rapidly becoming the most important tool for managing information in local government organizations. There can be no doubt that computing is here to stay, and that its use will continue to grow. As the technology moves ahead and new applications are developed, the opportunities for sophisticated computerized management of information will increase. Local governments cannot significantly influence the development of computing technology, but they can take care to make best use of the technology currently available. This chapter discusses several issues in using computing technology that are particularly important to local governments.[6]

A Note About Unsolved Problems in the Technology

> Despite a lack of policy research on certain areas of computing technology, decisions on these issues are critical and should be treated with great care.

There are many significant problems in efficient and productive use of computing technology. Unfortunately, research on some of these issues is either weak, irrelevant to local government, or lacking entirely. Therefore, it is worth noting those important issues which this chapter does *not* discuss.

First, there is no evaluation of the technical characteristics of specific pieces of hardware or software. For example, there is no discussion of whether

---

[6]Detailed discussions of these issues can be found in Volume 2, Part IV of this book, and in the EPRIS project report *Computing Technology and Information Management Policy*, by Richard D. Hackathorn, available from the National Technical Information Service.

it is more advantageous to use an IBM 370/155 running under VS-2 as compared to a 360/50 running under OS. Evaluations of this kind are not present in the research, and the literature provided by vendors is usually not comparative, and may be too biased to be considered objective. Nevertheless, choice of computing equipment or vendor is extremely important and should never be done hastily. The costs of a poor choice can be drastic.

Second, there is no discussion of the comparative technical advantages of batch vs. interactive computing. There has been no research comparing the advantages of either in live situations. There are certainly differences in utility of batch and interactive systems under different computing requirements, but these differences show up more in non-technical areas such as management, personnel, and so on. Since some kinds of computer equipment cannot handle interactive computing very well, it is recommended that a local government determine its needs for interactive computing before a choice of equipment is made.

Finally, there is no discussion of optimal configurations of computing capacity for various applications. This issue is hotly disputed due to differences in approaches taken in various software configurations, and there is little objective, useful research into the subject. Predetermination of need for equipment is a major area of investigation in computer science at the present, and it is likely that some answers will soon be forthcoming. Nevertheless, local goverment managers should be aware that computer vendors, as the major sources of computer advice to cities and counties, sometimes tend to recommend systems with substantial excess capacity. This, of course, sells larger computers. Local governments should be sure to get at least one separate, objective evaluation of computing requirements before following the advice of a vendor.

The Current Technology and What It Means

> Computing technology offers great payoffs for both effectiveness and efficiency in some local government operations, but these payoffs can only be realized if the technology is fully understood and exploited.

Computing technology, like any sophisticated technology, is complex and exacting. It is built upon physical, mathematical, logical and engineering sciences that are understood only by highly trained experts. To many untrained observers, computers are baffling "black boxes" capable of doing nearly anything. Yet even a small amount of experience with computing will show the observer that a computer's abilities, while impressive, are nonetheless limited.

Because computers are complex, they must be managed, programmed, and operated by people with sound training and experience. And because they are an expensive technology, inefficient or ineffective use of computers is costly. Therefore, it is important that local government management become versed in details of computer function, at least to the extent that the computer's basic abilities, limitations, and technical shortcomings are clear. Computing technology can be a great boon to local government operations; or it can be a costly headache. A great deal depends on willingness of local government management to learn what the technology is, does, and means in operational and management terms.

Several of the issues discussed in this chapter are presently "future issues" for many local governments. In other words, the issues have not yet become real concerns. This is either because a particular technology itself is new, or because the technology is just now getting out to users. This is particularly true of minicomputer technology, distributed network computing, and data base management. These three technologies have potential for great impact on local government data processing, and are included for that reason. Moreover, much current promotional literature deals with these concepts. They should be considered carefully, particularly by those local governments planning long-range data processing development. Nevertheless, most local governments should concentrate their evaluations on computing technology that is available now, and proven in action.

Strategy for Use of Computing Technology

Local governments should concentrate on managing information through use of technology, and not on managing the technology alone.

The purpose of a computerized information system is to *assist* in managing information; it should not be an end in itself. Local government management should recognize information technoloy as a tool to help information. This requires two things: a broad management perspective for controlling the technology, and at least one person knowledgeable about all the important aspects of information management to assist in making policy about use of the technology. This person, who may be a consultant if necessary, should be aware of current developments in technologies that might be applied to local government needs, particularly system building techniques, data base management, distributed computing, and geoprocessing.

System Building

Local governments should arrange the order in which they make system building decisions so as to place purchase of computing hardware last.

Local government decision makers are frequently presented with decisions on computing equipment and expenditures before they deliberate the important aspects of data handling and use. In many cases the first consideration for local governments getting into data processing or upgrading a current system has been to look at available equipment. After the computer is selected, an operating system and input/output software are selected (or are prescribed by the vendor) for use on the machine. Finally, those who are making the procurement decisions address the issue of data management and try to develop or purchase applications software that will do what they need on the equipment and operating system they have.

Since the purpose of using computers in data processing is to assist successful management of data, this traditional approach is somewhat backwards. It is a little like choosing an automobile without knowing what road conditions it will be used on, what performance and economy requirements it should meet, or how many people it must carry. Since the range of available passenger vehicles is large, from Volkswagens to Greyhound buses, such a premature decision would be foolish. Yet this is all too common in building a data processing system.

It is advisable for any local government to consider data processing development by use of a "reverse approach" to system building (see Figure 9). Instead of moving from machinery up to need, it is wiser to move from need down to machinery. Like automobiles, computer systems vary greatly in performance, capacity, ruggedness, and price. Some kinds of machines will not handle certain software or languages, and some machines do common tasks with greater speed and efficiency than others.

A more sensible system building procedure is to first consider what kind of data management applications the organization desires, and to explore available data management software and select those examples that will meet those needs. The next decision is to select an operating system and input/output software that will support these data management applications. Finally, only after these selections is it appropriate to select from a range of hardware systems that will meet the operating requirements of the data management software, and that will function with appropriate operating system software.

Data Base Management

Local governments experienced with EDP should consider using the data base management approach as a means of accomplishing information management.

A data base management system is to a data base what an operating system is to a computer. An operating system is the mechanism that controls and orders execution of tasks in the computer. A data base management

FIGURE 9

Information Management Pyramid

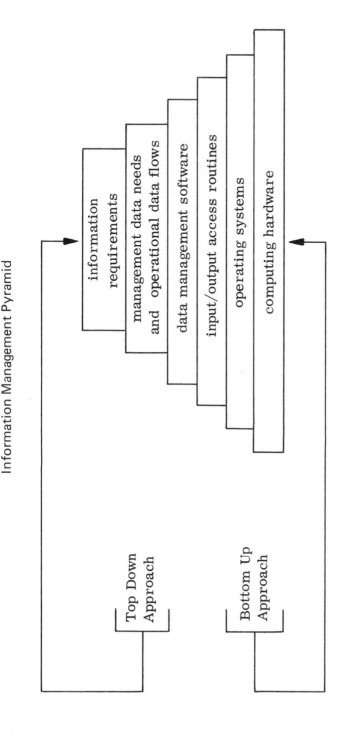

information
requirements

management data needs
and operational data flows

data management software

input/output access routines

operating systems

computing hardware

Top Down
Approach

Bottom Up
Approach

Source: Compiled by the authors, based on an original in R. D. Hackathorn, *Computing Technology and Information Management Policy*. Springfield, Va: National Technical Information Service, 1975.

system controls operations on data elements held in the data base. The data base management approach has come about in the last few years due to improvements in hardware and software, and decreases in per-unit costs of computing.

Data base management is rapidly gaining ground as a replacement for the older file management approach to computing. In file management, data are formed into files intended for a specific use in a specific program, often in batch operation. Data are usually "frozen" into these files, and cannot be used in other programs without being reworked. In data base management, data are made more independent of particular programs by use of special software. The same data element can be used in numerous programs, and therefore can serve multiple needs. Data base management promises greater flexibility and utility than the file management approach, especially for local governments hoping to move into more management- and planning-oriented uses of the computer.

Despite the advantages of data base management, it is wise to be aware of some common problems. The technology for data base management is relatively new, and therefore is not fully developed. There is very little research advice on how to arrive at an informed decision about whether to use data base management in given situations, yet the decision has important policy and cost implications. If a decision is made to development data base management capability, the best advice taken from the literature recommends the following guidelines:

1. Proceed slowly, studying all considerations thoroughly.
2. Plan development carefully, using benchmarks and milestones.
3. Use a phased, incremental development strategy.
4. Implement the design along functional lines (e.g., payroll, tax records, etc.).
5. Implement first on batch processes.
6. Implement first on small, non-critical applications.

Obtaining Data Base Management Capability

Local governments should use a commercially available data base management system rather than trying to develop one in-house.

Developing a data base management system is a very complex, expensive, time consuming task. Estimates of development and debugging costs for large data base management systems run into millions of dollars and man-years of time. Maintenance costs for these systems are high, and new software or hardware changes can render a system inoperable. Therefore, most local governments should not consider trying to develop their own data base management system.

Most manufacturers have data base management systems that are built specially for their machines. Generally speaking, these systems seem to work out well enough. Of course, the cost for these systems can be quite substantial, and some vendors insist on upgrading the organization's current computer before implementing a data base management system. Sometimes this expansion cost is justified, sometimes it is not. Careful exploration of alternatives is advised. Sometimes better arrangements for data management systems can be made through independent software vendors who offer such systems for use on common machines such as IBM 370.

If a local government decides to adopt a data base management system, it should seriously consider using one that comes close to the CODASYL standards. Although official standards for data base management systems are some years off, the CODASYL standards are comprehensive and carefully developed, and do offer a yardstick for measuring the capabilities of data base management systems.

Minicomputers

Local governments should consider using minicomputer systems to handle certain data processing requirements due to their flexibility and low purchase cost.

Computers used to be characterized by large arrays of expensive electronic equipment requiring huge amounts of electricity and air conditioning. Minicomputers are changing that image. Minicomputers using the latest technology of integrated circuitry, semiconductor memory, and virtual memory offer high computing speed, large capacity, and great flexibility at a much lower cost than larger machines now used in most local government data processing.[7] A city of 25,000 people could probably meet most of its data processing needs using a minicomputer system costing less than $100,000, including operating software (but not application software). This is about one-tenth the price of a "small" large computer system.

Most minicomputers are now equipped to handle common computing languages useful in local government data processing, such as FORTRAN and COBOL, and some have even been equipped with data base management systems. Development projects in geocoding, graphics and mapping, and other government data processing activities are now being conducted using mini-

---

[7]Examples of large computers commonly used in local governments are IBM 360s and 370s, UNIVAC 1100s, and NCR Century computers. Examples of minicomputers now being used in local governments are Digital Equipment PDP-11s, Data General NOVAs, and Hewlett-Packard 2100s.

computers. Some local governments have moved major portions of their EDP activity onto minicomputers.

Although "macrocomputers" will always be needed for very large computing jobs, such as analysis and simulation using large amounts of data, minicomputers will probably be used more and more by local governments to meet their data processing needs. There is as yet little research on government use of minicomputers, so there is no policy recommendation about their use, but local governments should nevertheless be aware of the importance of this technology for the future of their data processing activities.

Distributed vs. Centralized Computing Configurations

Due to improvements and developments in data communication, data base management, networking, and minicomputers, local governments should recognize that distributed computing is becoming a viable alternative to centralized computing.

It has been a long-standing assumption among computing professionals that large, centralized systems offer a maximum efficiency and effectiveness. This is being challenged by distributed computing, a technique brought about by advances in computer and software technology. Centralized systems were advantageous in the past when per-unit costs of computing power were very high. Large systems offered economies of scale, and made centralization advantageous. Now, however, with the introduction of powerful but relatively inexpensive minicomputers, that economy of scale has diminished. Already, the cost of the actual computer processor has become less than half the cost of most computer systems. The expensive hardware items are now peripherals and storage devices, and the most expensive item of all may soon be software.

Distributed computing entails moving computer processing, in whole or major part, out to the locations where most transactions occur. In effect, each major user can conceivably have its own minicomputer system, complete with its own data base. In the near future networking technology will enable computers at user locations to be connected to one another in order to share data and computing power. Networking is still in the developmental stages, though some experiments with networked minicomputer systems are now being carried out in local governments.

As with minicomputers, the technology of distributed computing is not discussed in the research literature. Nevertheless, local governments should consider the potential advantages of distributed systems, particularly when formulating long-range data processing plans.

Geoprocessing

Due to the special functions they perform, local governments stand to gain from expanded uses of geoprocessing techniques in support of planning and decision making.

Local governments are tied to geographic entities such as city boundaries, land parcels, streets, voter districts, and police precincts that define and contain their activities. In the past ten years there have been many developments in techniques of collecting, storing, analyzing, and presenting data linked to these geographic entities. Use of computers in this geoprocessing activity has grown substantially, and now is one of the most important developing areas of computer use in local governments.

The utility of geoprocessing comes mainly from applying the capabilities of the computer to managing and processing data according to common geographic identifiers. For example, geoprocessing techniques can be used to help manage property taxation by linking tax records, addresses, and property owners' names to land parcels. Numerous counties and cities are now using geoprocessing in this way. Other possibilities for use are analysis of population movements within metropolitan areas, studies of transportation activity and need, analysis of voter performance and attitudes by voting district, and allocation of policy and firefighting forces.

The research indicates several recommendations to local governments undertaking geoprocessing activities. First, it is very advantageous if local agencies in the same area can make use of each other's geographic base data. This necessitates a common base map for use among all local agencies. Therefore, local agencies should agree to use of such a common base map for coding geographic data. Second, the literature recommends that this map be used on the state plane coordinate system. This system is fully documented, its coordinates follow county lines, and over 30 states use it to record property deeds. Third, data base management offers potential for new capabilities in managing and linking geographic base files, so it is wise to consider both geoprocessing and data base management together.

Evaluating the Computer's Performance

The technical performance of computer systems should be periodically reviewed to see if the system is performing up to specification and to assess possible needs for expanding or upgrading the system.

Reliable and efficient hardware performance is a necessity if a computer system is to offer maximum potential as a tool for data management. Therefore, periodic evaluations should be performed to insure hardware performance expectations are being met. In addition, these evaluations provide an opportunity to consider upgrading the current system by adding capacity or adopting new technological developments if need warrants.

Rapid advancements in the field of information systems present both blessings and problems for local government information system managers. New developments frequently provide previously unavailable capability, but they are expensive and often incompatible with existing older equipment. The executive must therefore be sure that any new development is evaluated for implementation on the basis of what it can realistically provide given its cost. Local governments should attempt to capitalize on any new technological developments that will significantly improve their information services, and should avoid adopting developments that are too esoteric, are incompatible with their present systems, or simply are not needed.

Summary

The technical aspects of a computerized information system are fundamental to the system's utility to the organization. As with any modern, technology-based enterprise, a computerized information system rests upon a technical foundation. It is essential for local government executives to have at least a rudimentary understanding of the technology if sound, reasonable policies for computerized information systems are to be made. The responsibility for effective and efficient control and operation of a computerized information system rests on management. If a government expects to get full benefit from its computer resource, top executives and departmental managers must have a good understanding of what computers can do and where the government stands with respect to the current state of the art in computing. Moreover, data processing managers should be well-versed in both current and forthcoming computer technologies, and be able to communicate the implications of these to other managers.

The recommendations of this chapter can be summarized in eight points:

1. Computer technology must be fully understood by those who manage it if it is to be used to maximum utility.

2. Executive emphasis should be placed on controlling the technology as a tool in the larger context of information management, and not on controlling the technology alone.

3. The system building process should be approached by first considering data needs, then data management software then an operating system, and finally computer hardware, instead of the other way around.

4. When planning for later EDP activity, local governments should investigate use of data base management to achieve information control. If a local government decides to obtain data base management capability, it should procure a commercially available system rather than build one in-house.

5. Local governments should seriously consider using minicomputers to meet some or all of their data processing needs.

6. Due to advancements in technology, distributed computing will offer certain advantages over centralized hardware. Local governments should consider distributed configurations in their plans for data processing development or expansion.

7. Local governments should explore the benefits of geoprocessing as a tool for information management in local agencies, but should exercise caution to avoid adopting any geoprocessing system prematurely.

8. Evaluation of computer performance should be done periodically.

8

DISCLOSURE
AND PRIVACY
CONCERNS

Local governments have been assigned basic record-keeping functions for the orderly functioning of community and society. Births, deaths, marriages, divorces, arrests, property exchanges, and many other events and transactions are recorded by local government as a service to citizens and to other governments. Local governments, like their federal and state counterparts, must have certain basic information o individuals if they are to perform services and collect revenues to support their services. Today, many local governments require accurate and current information on income, property ownership, residence, voter registration, school-age children, criminal history, and so on. As the role of government in maintaining order and providing direct services increases, the need for personal information on citizens increases as well. Today, governments are the largest collectors of personal information on individuals.

In recent years, a concern for the privacy of individuals has arisen in the face of the collection and use of personal information by governments. Fueled by both fact and fiction, predictions of suppressive control of the individual by the government have emerged. More often than not, these predictions refer to the existence of computerized files of personal data as threats to individual freedom. Computerization of personal data did not create this "privacy problem"; it merely called attention to a new aspect of an old problem: the tradeoff between government's need to know certain information about individuals, and the individual's desire to maintain personal privacy by withholding information. This chapter explores some important elements in the privacy and disclosure issue that are particularly related to information systems in local government.[8]

The Nature of Privacy

There is no complete definition of privacy that can be applied to all situations, so the term must be applied in the context of individual and community standards.

The concept "privacy" is almost impossible to define precisely. Among individual people, privacy can refer to any number of states from total seclusion to total social interaction. In most societies and communities there are accepted boundaries for privacy, but even these vary from place to place. In the United States the term "privacy" has long been identified with individualism and personal freedom. The traditions and customs of the United States have upheld the right of a person to withdraw from society. From a legal standpoint, privacy is inseparably tied to concepts such as slander and libel, and has had the status of a grounds for civil suit. There are many successful suits for "invasion of privacy" on the case books, and in recent years several states have passed legislation making privacy a constitutional right.

But what is privacy? Research indicates that people have several definitions they attach to the word. The first is "spatial privacy," that is, the desire to be away from the physical presence of other people. The second is "personal privacy," related more to the desire to maintain personal thoughts, activities and expression, with no fear of assault or harassment. The third is "information privacy," or the desire of an individual to withhold information on himself because he does not want others to have it. Most legal actions involving privacy have been related to spatial and personal privacy, but the growing interest in information privacy may change that.

Clearly, concern for privacy in the context of information systems and data bases emphasizes information privacy. Concern about information privacy varies from community to community and from time to time. It is based, among other things, on personal and religious beliefs of the citizens, on local traditions, on reactions to recent events, and on citizen faith and trust in government. Therefore, any reasonable consideration of privacy issues in a community must include an understanding of community attitudes toward the subject.

---

[8]More detailed discussion of the issues raised here can be found in Volume 2, Part V of this book, and in the EPRIS project report, *Disclosure, Privacy, and Information Management Policy* by Frances I. Mossman and John Leslie King, available from the National Technical Information Service.

Privacy, like other important social issues such as civil rights and equal employment opportunity, must be considered in the context of local values. This fact makes agreement on the issue difficult to achieve. Still, like other complex social issues requiring local governments attention, the privacy issue must be dealt with affirmatively. Federal and state governments are now beginning to require local governments to meet privacy standards by drafting legislation concerning personal information in local government files. The vagueness of the definition of privacy leads most legislators to favor laws that watchdog citizen privacy rights. This is probably a good thing, since citizens are more vulnerable to abuse than are organizations that hold records on them, including local governments. However, this means that current and pending legislation will have a major impact on many data collection and record-keeping practices of local governments.

Local government executives must realize that despite the vagueness and uncertainty about the nature of privacy, public concern will bring specific legislation to control all government activities involving personal information.

Federal and State Legislation[9]

Federal and state privacy legislation may drastically affect local government information practices, so it is wise for local policymakers to keep abreast of and provide input to development of such legislation.

Numerous pieces of legislation aimed at controlling collection, storage, and use of personal information have been passed by Congress and state legislators. More are on the floor now, or are being prepared. Much of this legislation impacts local governments. For example, one federal law has recently been enacted to require school districts receiving federal money to open all student records to students and their parents. Another law prohibits government agencies at all levels from withholding services to individuals if they refuse to give their social security number (except as required by the Social Security Administration and the Internal Revenue Service). Such legislation is important to local governments.

Local policymakers should keep close watch on all such legislation. A simple requirement in a federal law can have drastic effects on a local government's record-keeping and data collection activity. For example, a law recently proposed in the State of California would require all public agencies to give

[9]The study that gave rise to this section of this book was completed shortly before passage of the Privacy Act of 1974. This Act, in particular, is very important in the area of privacy legislation, and contains a number of provisions of interest to local governments.

an individual written notice of all files on him in those agencies, and would require another notice of every use made of that data. Such a requirement would burden public agencies with enormous costs for compliance. Unless local agencies inform their federal and state representatives about their concerns, the needs of local government may be overlooked. It is recommended that a member of the local government staff be assigned the responsibility for following privacy legislation in the state and federal government.

Disclosure and Privacy

The privacy of individuals and the disclosure of information vital to public interest must be balanced carefully to permit proper function of government while insuring personal rights.

Privacy of information and disclosure of information are contrary. Maximum personal privacy usually entails minimal disclosure of personal information to others. Since local governments cannot perform their duties without at least some disclosure of personal information, the need for individual information privacy must be offset by the need for disclosure of information in the public interest. Disclosure is as controversial as privacy nowadays. Laws have been passed to "open up" the affairs of government and to expose the financial affiliations of government officials. Campaign disclosure requirements and preappointment investigations submit many public officials to intense public scrutiny. These disclosure requirements are enforced in the public interest to help prevent those with conflicting interests or questionable past activities from getting into positions where they might abuse the public trust.

Other disclosures of personal information required by governments serve the public in various ways. Disclosure of property tax assessments helps prevent unfair taxation practice. Disclosure of court and arrest records protects both society and the individual: society has a record of past dispositions against a person, and the person has a public account of a disposition of trial or arrest to protect himself from double jeopardy. Indeed, some legislators argue that sealing arrest records from public scrutiny would open the door to abuse of police power.

There are serious consequences to extremes of disclosure and privacy. On the one hand, by restricting required disclosures of personal data, much of the useful information now available to governmental officials and agencies might be buried. Effective law enforcement might become more difficult. Tax assessment would be open to abuse. Those with power and influence would be better able to "manipulate the system behind the scenes" than would the poor and non-influential. On the other hand, forced disclosure of personal information can amount to unnecessary surveillance and lead to dangerous social consequences. Individuals can lose faith in their government, and the government can gain inordinate powers at the expense of personal liberties.

Striking the balance between privacy and disclosure is not easy, but it is necessary. Every decision about either privacy or disclosure policy must be made in light of its wider effects. Once again, privacy is a matter of social and personal values, so governmental need for information must be tempered to conform to that need as well as to meet the demands of government operations.

Dealing with Privacy: A Management Concern

The responsibility for insuring protection of individual privacy in local government record-keeping activity rests on local government executives and managers. They must face privacy issues and deal with them conscientiously.

Local government executives and managers must realize that they are responsible for insuring against privacy problems that arise from local government record-keeping. Due to the social and political seriousness of civil rights issues like privacy, this ultimate responsibility should not be delegated to others. The whole issue of privacy is real and very volatile. More than one high local government official has been called to task for the questionable record-keeping and information practices of subordinate department heads.

Privacy and disclosure problems for executives can arise from two directions. The problem of misuse of personal data is obvious, and executives should take every step to prevent abuse. But another problem is the use of the importance of privacy matters to cover up improper data and record-keeping uses. For example, under the guise of protecting the privacy of individuals named in a file, a department can conceal the fact that the file contains data that should never have been collected in the first place. This has happened in several local governments.

Perhaps the strongest recommendation provided by research in the privacy and disclosure area is that managers and policymakers keep a close eye on the record-keeping and data collection activities of their organizations. By being both sensitive to the concerns of individuals and aware of record-keeping practices within the organization, many confrontations about privacy and disclosure issues can be avoided to everyone's satisfaction.

Policy for Privacy and Disclosure

Local government policymakers should establish privacy policies that are in line with community attitudes, and that insure as free a flow of information as possible.

Local governments should establish privacy policies that deal comprehensively with all personal data held in a government's data files. Only comprehensive policy, covering all personal information, will provide complete top management control over data activities involving sensitive personal information. This policy should contain three things: (1) a clear statement of the local government's philosophy about privacy and personal information; (2) specific guidelines and rules surrounding collection, storage, use, and dissemination of personal information; and (3) procedures whereby citizens can seek correction of errors and restitution for abuses. In particular, the policy should be very specific about what kinds of data are not to be collected, and about who has authority to see what kinds of sensitive information. This may necessitate establishing categories of personal data, such as "sensitive police intelligence data" or "restricted-access welfare classification data." This, of course, will depend on the characteristics of the local government involved. Further detail on classification schemes for personal data can be found in Volume 2, Part V.

Privacy and disclosure policies should be developed publicly. Citizens should be invited and encouraged to participate in the policymaking process. The policies should contain provisions for amendment and change as needed. Above all, the policies should reflect the balance between community desires for privacy and the government's legitimate need for personal information. This means that in addition to relevant local government participants, such as the city attorney, data processing manager, chief of police and so on, the policymaking committee should include representatives of minority groups, civil liberties organizations, and other community organizations concerned with privacy and citizen's rights.

Provisions for Citizen Input

> Local governments should consider establishing a policy and review board made up of both government and community interests to oversee government information practices, and to handle citizen complaints.

Once a policy on privacy and disclosure of personal information in local government data banks has been developed, the policy must be implemented, enforced, and adapted as needed. It is recommended that local governments establish a review board to serve this function. This board should be made up of representatives from all interested and relevant government and community concerns. The board's purpose is to review information practices, to recommend and/or make changes in the policy as needed, and to serve as a sounding board for resolving citizen complaints.

Research into the effectiveness of such policy and review boards in the privacy area is sparse, but available experiences of local governments who have tried them provide some direction and advice.

First, since this board must provide a full perspective on the privacy and disclosure issue, it is essential that it be made up of individuals who truly represent a cross-section of the community. Second, the members should have a genuine interest in privacy, and should have a willingness to work for betterment of both individual rights and local government operations. Finally, the board should be given the authority to act as it sees need. Without such authority, the board will not serve a true review and evaluation function.

Dealing with Data Security

Local governments should make every effort to insure that files containing personal information be secured against access and uses prohibited by the policy on privacy and disclosure.

Any personal information classified as sensitive (that is, to be seen only by authorized persons) should be stored in such a way to make it safe from unauthorized access. In addition, all personal information, whether it is sensitive or not, should be protected from unauthorized alteration or removal. Therefore, any local government information system containing personal information should have rigid security protection.

Security of record information has been a problem since long before computers came on the scene, but computers introduce new considerations. Properly managed and protected, a computer offers great security for information. Yet, if the security is broken, computerized information can be collected, altered, or deleted on a much larger scale and in a much shorter time than information in a manual system. Proper security of the information system itself entails safeguards such as locked doors, pass gates, security patrols, and so on. Proper security of the data in the system includes use of "password" or other access controls, protection of communication lines from wiretaps, safe storage of storage discs and tapes, radiation shielding, and so on. These safeguards should be geared to the need for security at the installation.

The Future of the Privacy Issue

It is likely that future legislation and public concern will demand more careful supervision of collection, use, and dissemination of personal information. Local governments should take care to plan for this when formulating long range plans for data practices.

If any single fact shines from the collected research on privacy, it is this: privacy and disclosure problems are too important and too complex to tackle on a piecemeal basis. The intricate balance between individual needs for privacy and the society's requirements for information is not clearly understood, but it must be considered in regulating the behavior of both individuals and organizations toward mutually desirable goals. Only a clear recognition of the complexity of the privacy problem will allow formulation of sensible policy.

Local governments will probably be called on to take greater care in their information practices in the future. New legislation and growing public concern for privacy will call into question records practices that have been carried in one form or another for a long time. At the same time, increasing responsibilities of governments to meet social needs will require more personal information on individuals. This paradox can only be resolved if local government takes a decisive, responsible role in dealing with privacy and disclosure issues. Therefore, local governments should begin now to plan future information practices with measures to insure that privacy and disclosure needs are met.

Summary

The privacy and disclosure issue is the most politically loaded of all issues in local government information systems. It involves personal beliefs and attitudes, legal complexities, and problems of community values, as well as administrative and technical concerns. Local government executives must accept and deal with the reality of the privacy issue. If privacy has not yet become a topic of serious debate in many local governments, it will as populations grow, as cities and urban areas become denser, and as government information activities are called into question. This chapter has presented some recommendations for dealing with privacy and disclosure issues in local governments. These recommendations can be summarized in six points.

1. Privacy means different things to different people, so it must be interpreted in light of community values. Nevertheless, it must be dealt with affirmatively as an important social issue.

2. Local governments should keep close track of federal and state privacy and disclosure legislation that may affect them.

3. Protection of individual privacy must be carefully balanced with legitimate societal needs for personal information. In local government, management must take responsibility and initiative in assuring both needs are met as well as possible.

4. A comprehensive, thoughtful policy, developed with citizen input, is necessary to insure management control over local government information practice. Once this policy is formulated, it should be monitored, adapted, and enforced by a review board made up of all relevant interests.

5. Steps should be taken to insure that all personal data in local government custody is secure and safe from unauthorized intrusion or abuses.

6. Local governments should begin to include provisions for proper security and privacy in their plans for future information activities.

9

CONCLUSION:
URBAN
INFORMATION
SYSTEMS
AS A FIELD
OF STUDY

The preceding eight chapters address a number of important policy issues in the field of computerized information systems as applied to local governments based on findings from policy-relevant research in the area. The discussions of these issues are intended to be of value to executive, managerial, and staff personnel concerned with policymaking about the use of modern computing technology in local governments. Yet, anyone who is familiar with computerized information systems in government will find that some important issues are either covered lightly or are excluded entirely from this discussion due to a lack of useful research. This lack of research is a problem that plagues the field of urban information systems, and makes attempts at study and synthesis difficult.

The concluding chapter of this volume is devoted to a discussion of urban information systems as a field of study. The attempt here is to focus attention on the problems that the field faces, and to discuss what should be done to alleviate those problems. This subject is as important for executives and managers as it is for those in academic and government institutions who study information technology and set policy for its uses. In the next few years the use of computing will expand, both in terms of the number of government organizations using it, and the kinds of activities computerized. If the technology is to be used efficiently, effectively, and to the best of its potential in the service of public policymaking and management, the serious shortcomings in the state of knowledge about development and use of computing must be alleviated.

The Problem of Identity

The various disciplines that have a part in Urban Information Systems design, development, use, and study should bind together in multi-discipli-

nary study efforts to provide a unified perspective and establish an identity
for the field.

Most people familiar with urban administration understand the term
"urban information systems" in a general way, but as a field of study the
subject has weak identity. This is because an urban information system, just
like any other system of social and technical components, is an amalgam of
different professional fields. Urban information systems come about through
the efforts of computer scientists, engineers, urban executives, managers, businessmen, politicians, technicians, planners, and a host of other participants.
An urban information system spans many professional boundaries to link
managers, analysts, technicians, users, policymakers, vendors, and others together in a common enterprise. And these systems usually span organizational
boundaries within governments because they serve as common resources and
facilities for numerous departments and agencies.

Taken together, these characteristics make the field of urban information
systems a bit of a hodge-podge. Since different professional interests are involved, different kinds of study issues are raised. Public administrators study
the effects of computerized information systems on such things as decisionmaking and departmental performance. Political scientists study the impacts
of these systems on the political characteristics of organizations. Sociologists
study the impacts on people and organizational structures. Computer scientists
study the way computing is used to perform tasks, and how well the technology serves its intended purpose.

Such fragmentation of study is understandable since the field is so young.
And in some ways, this diverse interest in urban information systems is desirable because it focuses the attention of many experts on important issues in
the use of the technology for public purposes. But because people in these
disciplines usually maintain intellectual and organizational boundaries, and
seldom cross into each other's "turf," the field as a whole has remained
fragmented and undefined. This presents little problem to people who are
concerned only with a single perspective on the subject, but it is a major
stumbling block to those who wish to understand urban information systems
in full perspective. And it is particularly troublesome for people like policymakers and executives who need guidance to deal with information systems
as complete entities involving hardware, software, people, and organizations.

The problem of establishing an identity for the field of urban information
systems *as* a field will be alleviated when more effort is put into research using
multi-disciplinary study teams. As the roles, uses, and payoffs related to computerized activities in organizations become better understood in the broader
perspective of public policy and administration, the field of urban information
systems will become more defined. This, in turn, will help to focus attention
on the more complex and important problems in harnessing computer technology to serve local government's needs.

Research vs. Development

> Research, evaluation, and documentation must become integral parts of all
> development efforts in order to gain maximum payoff from development
> funds. Results of research and evaluation must be disseminated to those who
> stand to gain from such documentation.

A second major problem in the urban information systems field has been
a tendency in the past to undertake development efforts in the name of research. Although the terms "research" and "development" are often used
together, they are not synonymous. A research effort seeks to uncover what
is not presently known and to make sense of that new knowledge in light of
what is already known. A development effort takes new or existing knowledge
and attempts to put it to work in some way. Of course, both activities overlap-
-for example, many of the people who first researched the theories of atomic
fission were also instrumental in developing the first atomic reactor. And even
today, some of these same people are actively involved in research to find ways
to prevent nuclear warfare and other atomic disasters. Nevertheless, research
and development should not be confused.

There have been many developmental efforts in urban information systems in recent years. Most of the $200 million per year the federal government
has contributed to information systems in local government over the last ten
years has been for development. These efforts have produced successes and
failures. Some of the agencies doing development have built themselves very
useful, efficient systems; others have found themselves shackled with expensive
"white elephants" that cost as much to get rid of as they do to keep.

Due to their enormous expense, development projects are practical only
if others have the opportunity to copy successes and avoid mistakes. Unfortunately, however, both successful and unsuccessful efforts have usually gone
undocumented. Despite the large number of unsuccessful development efforts,
it is nearly impossible to find clear, useful analyses of *why* these efforts failed.
Even worse, successful developments are seldom documented carefully enough
to allow others to achieve equal success. This situation has cost untold millions
of dollars in unnecessary duplication of development efforts, and has retarded
successful use of the technology in many locations.

Much of the effort put into development would have been more worthwhile if it had been put into evaluation research. In particular, there is a need
for research into how computing is actually used in organizations, what makes
for success or failure in development of computerized information systems,
and what real benefits accrue to organizations that use these systems. This does
not mean that development should be replaced with research--in fact, development is essential to progress in the field. Rather, development and research
efforts should be linked, and in some cases united, to make best use of develop-

ment and research funds. Large scale developmment projects offer an excellent opportunity for research, since any development is in some sense an experiment. Stronger requirements for evaluation and documentation in development projects will help reduce this problem, and a dedication to sharing the results of both successes and failures will greatly improve the utility of those results to others.

Problems in Support for Research, Development, and Training

> There should be increased support for continuous and coordinated research, development, and training in the field, preferably through establishment of centers for that purpose.

Many of the shortcomings in research and literature on urban information systems are the results of problems in support of research, development, and training activities in the field. From the federal government alone, support for these activities has come at various times from the National Science Foundation, the National Bureau of Standards, the Law Enforcement Assistance Administration, and various cabinet departments such as Housing and Urban Development, Transportation, Defense, and Health, Education and Welfare. Universities and private foundations have provided research and training. State governments have supported development and training efforts at the local level, and of course, local governments have undertaken the largest share of this activity on their own.

The eclectic nature of support for research, development, and training has resulted in several problems. First, support has not been continuous from the different agencies, and many worthwhile projects have been cut off before they could produce worthwhile results. Second, there has been little cooperation to improve dissemination among the various agency-supported projects, thereby making findings difficult for users to locate. Third, there have been no standard training criteria because there has been little interaction among the organizations that do research and those that train future practitioners. Finally, there is no overall direction to the field's development which might be provided if research and development support were more coordinated and stabilized.

Cooperation is needed between organizations doing research, development, and training in the field. More important, cooperation is needed among those agencies and organizations that fund and support research, development, and training. There have been notable attempts at cooperation among funding agencies, as in the case of the urban information systems Inter-agency Committee (the USAC Program) which was made up of representatives of seven federal agencies. This kind of cooperative funding should be encouraged, provided that a commitment is made to reap the full evaluation benefits from the projects undertaken. Furthermore, centers for research, development, and training in information systems and public policy should be established to consolidate and coordinate efforts in the field. Two such centers are now developing, one at Harvard University and another in the Public Policy Research Organization at the University of California, Irvine. Portions of such centers also exist in Connecticut, Georgia, and Washington, D.C. Establishment and support of these centers should help reduce the problems caused by scattered and discontinuous research, development, and training activities.

Another model for various groups that support and conduct urban information systems research and development is provided by the Computer Utilization Group of the Organization for Economic Cooperation and Development (OECD). This group is comprised of representatives from member nations of the OECD, and coordinates research and study of commonly defined problems of interest in computing in the public sector. The group publishes its findings in the OECD Informatics Series--a set of documents that describe current work in the urban information systems field in terms both researchers and practitioners can relate to. Establishment of such a coordinating group for work on urban information systems in the U.S. would be a major contribution to improving the status and efficacy of the field.

Where the Field Should Go from Here

In the next few years greater emphasis will be placed on adopting technology to serve the needs of public policymakers and managers. Indeed, in the last five years there has been a dramatic increase in the kinds of technological assistance cities and counties have been willing to experiment with. In most cases these technological experiments have been conducted for the purpose of trying to save money, improve decisionmaking and planning, increase efficiency, and improve service delivery. Undoubtedly, the pressure to achieve these ends will grow in the future, so the need for reliable guidance in use of technology will increase as well. This volume has presented advice to policymakers and managers for making use of information technology, primarily computers. It is built on the assumption that the technology is here to stay, that the benefits of the technology can outweigh the costs, and that the technology can be brought to bear on pressing problems facing local governments in the United States.

Technology has costs as well as benefits, however. It is a foolish person who believes that technology is always equated with progress. In fact, many of the serious problems facing modern America come directly from technological developments. The automobile has brought air pollution, traffic congestion, and dependence on foreign sources for petroleum. Aerosols have brought the serious danger of environmental damage and climatic changes. Chemical fertilizers and pesticides have profoundly affected the delicate ecosystem that supports man and the other creatures he shares the world with. There can be no doubt that each technological advancement brings a new set of problems to deal with. Information technology is no different.

The direct costs of using information technology are readily apparent--the technology is expensive, it does not always do the job it is intended for, and so on. But the more subtle costs are only now beginning to appear. What is the societal cost of replacing or altering human labor with machine labor? What social dangers arise from storage of huge computerized files of personal information on citizens that could fall into the hands of tyrants? What does creation of a technology-dependent society do to our sense of values and purpose as a nation and people? These are all profound questions that must be dealt with honestly. We know that every technology bears a cost that must be anticipated ahead of time. In the future, the new field of urban information systems should go beyond the narrow interest in "how can a computer do this job?", to ask "*should* a computer be used to do this job?" and "who is this technology to serve--the leaders or the led?" These questions deserve the attention of every participant in research, development, training, and use of information technology in a modern world.

BIBLIOGRAPHY

MANAGERS' BIBLIOGRAPHY ON
URBAN INFORMATION SYSTEMS

This is an annotated bibliography of selected works related to computers and information systems. The works chosen are non-technical and intended for policymakers and managers who want a general introduction to the field or to specific topics discussed in this guide.

Volume 2 of this book, *A Review of the Research*, contains another bibliography, covering all of the works that were reviewed and cited in the EPRIS study. An extended bibliography also can be found in the EPRIS project report, *Project Bibliography and Research Abstracts*, available from the National Technical Information Service (PB 245696). This bibliography contains approximately 3,000 references, listings by author and subject, and research abstracts. The listings can be used to search for documents on selected topics, and the abstracts can be used to review the contents of each document.

California Intergovernmental Board on EDP. *Guidelines
for establishing requirements for security and confidentiality of information
systems*. Sacramento: State of California, Documents Section, January 1974.

This very readable report presents guidelines that will assist local officials in evaluating their current requirements for security and confidentiality of information and in developing a security plan.

California Intergovermental Board on Electronic Data
Processing, *Successful Development of EDP in California Government*. Sacramento: State of California, Documents Section, 1974.

This report provides guidelines, based upon the experience of local officials and data processing directors, for developing computer applications and managing EDP systems.

Canning, R. G., & Sisson, R. L. *The Management of Data
Processing*. New York: John Wiley and Sons, 1967.

This short book is one of the better written and and instructive guides to actual management of data processing. It is of particular value to those managers who have direct contact with or responsibility for EDP in the organization.

Colton, K. W. Police and computers: Use, acceptance
and impact of automation. *The Municipal Year Book*, 1972, *39*, 119-136.

This report contains data on the extent, pattern and impacts of computer use in police departments in cities.

Cooke, D. F. Geocoding and geographic base files: The
first four generations. San Francisco: American Institute of Planners, 1971.

This paper, delivered at an AIP conference, contains a good overview of approaches to geoprocessing and how they have evolved to the present.

Dial, O. E., & Goldberg, E. M. *Privacy, security, and
computers: Guidelines for municipal and other public information systems.*
New York: Praeger, 1974.

This is probably the most directly useful and relevant piece on privacy and computer concerns for local governments. It spells out in considerable detail the basic issues local governments must address regarding privacy and security in their information systems, and provides a number of sensible recommendations for actions local policy-makers might take to avoid privacy and security problems.

Downs, A. A realistic look at the final payoffs from
urban data systems, *Public Administration Review*, 1967, 27(3), 204-210.

This stimulating article distinguishes between power impacts and technical impacts from computerized information systems. It argues that the power impacts have generally been ignored and are potentially more significant than the technical impacts in determining "final payoffs," i.e., outcomes of decisions and action in the community.

Hearle, E. & Mason, R. J. *A data processing system for
state and local governments.* Englewood Cliffs: Prentice-Hall, 1963.

This book is considered the classic work on EDP in local government, and is still a good nontechnical introduction to the field. Although some of its concepts have not yet proven feasible, this work has had considerable influence on the field.

Kraemer, K. L. The evolution of information systems for
urban administration. *Public Administration Review*, 1969, 24(4), 389-462.

This essay traces the development of EDP in local government from 1950 to 1970, presents an overview of various approaches to using EDP, and critiques the experience with each approach. It ends with a call for more integrated approaches to developing EDP.

Kraemer, K. L., & King, J. L. *Computers, power and urban management: What every local executive should know.* Sage Professional Papers on Administrative and Policy Studies, Volume 3, 03-031, Beverly Hills, CA: Sage Publications, 1976.

This introductory essay argues that local government executives must take control of EDP rather than leave it to develop uncontrolled. It points out that the political and technical costs and benefits of computers and information systems greatly affect the executive's interest and the government interests as a whole. It outlines ten steps for executives to take charge of EDP.

Kraemer, K. L., Mitchell, W. H., Weiner, M. E., & Dial, O. E. *Integrated municipal information systems.* New York: Praeger Publishers, 1974.

This book essentially presents the USAC (Urban Information Systems Inter-Agency Committee) approach to developing EDP systems for local government. It expands upon the concepts and methods for developing integrated information systems, such as those sponsored by USAC in Charlotte, NC, Dayton, OH, Long Beach, CA and Wichita Falls, TX.

Leavitt, H. J. & Whisler, T. L. Management in the 1980's. *Harvard Business Review*, 1958, *36*(6), 41-48.

This classic essay contains extensive predictions about the impact of computers on organizations and management. Many of its predictions have been correct, some appear to have been in error, or at least have not yet occurred. It remains a provocative piece, well worth reading.

Newsweek. *Words of the Computer Age.* New York: American National Standards Institute, 1974.

This is a pocket-size glossary (larger than the one in this book) of terms used in electronic data processing. It is very handy for policy-makers and managers who are unfamiliar with terms in the field. It is more extensive than the glossary included in this volume.

Nolan, R. L. Computer data bases: The future is now. *Harvard Business Review*, 1973, *51*(5), 98-114.

This article is a good introduction to the concept of integrated systems (see also Pendleton), to data bases and data base management systems as means of implementing integrated systems, and to the consequences of these systems for managers and the information management throughout the organization.

Organization for Economic Co-operation and Development
   (OECD). *Automated information management in public administration.
   Present developments and impacts*. Paris: OECD, 1973.

   This fourth study of the Computer Utilization Group of the OECD contains
   an excellent discussion of the "information management" concept, the experience of selected countries with it, and some of the policy issues surrounding
   successful implementation of the concept.

Patrick, R. L. Computers and Information Flow. Santa
   Monica: The Rand Corporation, 1973. P-2791-2.

   This essay is an interesting and very readable introduction to computers and
   their uses which cleverly combines definition of terms with a broad perspective on EDP.

Pendleton, J. C. Integrated Information Systems. *AFIPS
   Fall Joint Computer Conference Proceedings*, 1971, *39*, 491-500.

   Although written for businessmen, this essay is an excellent introduction to
   the differences between integrated and independent information systems and
   what difference these two kinds of systems make for the managers of organizations.

Strickrod, R. L., & Martin, L. C. *Data processing analysis of costs, benefits, and resource
   allocations*. Lane County, OR: Lane County Management Report, February
   1973.

   This report presents a cost-benefit analysis of all then-operational computer
   applications in Lane County. It is one of the best existing examples of
   cost-benefit analysis of computerized systems in local government, although
   the methodology is flawed.

Thomas, U. Computerized data banks in public administration. Paris: Organization for Economic Cooperation and Development,
   1971.

   This report is the first in a series of ten from the Informatics Working Group
   of the OECD and it provides a broad perspective on the potential uses of
   computers in government and the policy issues raised by computer use.

U.S. Department of Health, Education & Welfare. *Records,
   computers and the rights of citizens*. Report of the Secretary's Advisory
   Committee on Automated Personal Data Systems. DHEW Pub. No. (OS)
   73-94. Washington, D.C.: U.S. Government Printing Office, July 1973.

This book summarizes most of the basic issues in the problem of privacy and government records on citizens. It is based on the work of a committee established by HEW in 1972 to assess the current state of record-handling activities in government and private organizatins, and to make recommendations on what might be done to insure protection of personal privacy regarding record-keeping. A lively, informative book.

Watlington, M. ADP in municipal government. *Urban Data Service*. Washington: International City Management Association, 1970, *2* (10), 1-16.

This report contains data on the extent and pattern of computer use in cities as of 1970.

Wright, J. Evaluating and developing an EDP system. *MIS report*. Washington, D.C.: International City Management Association, 1973.

This essay presents practical steps for evaluating the current status of EDP in a local government and for planning the future development of EDP systems. Although the essay is a good one, it tends to emphasize considerations related mainly to management uses rather than to operational uses.

PUBLICATIONS AND DOCUMENTS ON INFORMATION SYSTEMS FROM THE PUBLIC POLICY RESEARCH ORGANIZATION

The EPRIS Series on
Policy Related Research In Municipal Information Systems*
The full citation shown above should be used when ordering
any of these documents.

Kraemer, K. L., & King, J. L. *Volume I, Summary of research findings for policymakers.* (NTIS PB 245687).

Kraemer, K. L., Lucas, H. C., Hackathorn, R. D., & Emrey, R. C. *Volume II, Computer utilization in local government.* (NTIS PB 245688).

Schrems, E., & Duggar, G. S. *Volume III, Information systems procurement, computer resource allocation, and finance policy.* (NTIS PB 245689).

Hackathorn, R. D. *Volume IV, Computing technology and information management policy.* (NTIS PB 245689).

Mossman, F. I., & King, J. L. *Volume V, Disclosure, privacy, and information policy.* (NTIS PB 245691).

Sartore, A., & Kraemer, K. L. *Volume VI, Automation, work, and manpower policy.* (NTIS PB 245689).

Matthews, J. R. *Volume VII, Information functions, services, and administrative policy.* (NTIS PB 245693).

King, J. L., & Kraemer, K. L. *Volume VIII, Policy concerns in municipal information systems: Results of a Delphi experiment.* (NTIS PB 245694).

---

*These reports are available from:
National Technical Information Service (NTIS)
U.S. Department of Commerce
5285 Port Royal Road
Springfield, VA 22161

Kraemer, K. L., & King, J. L. *Volume IX, Methodology for*
evaluation of research in municipal information systems. (NTIS PB 245695).

Matthews, J. R., & Smith, S. O. *Volume X, Project*
bibliography and research abstracts. (NTIS PB 245696). Other

Publications of the Urban Information Systems
Research Group

Danziger, J. N. Executives see trend to more sophistication. *County News*, 1975, *7*(40), pp. 10, 13.

Danziger, J. N. EPD's diverse impacts on local governments.
Nation's Cities, 1975, *13*(10), 24-27.

Danziger, J. N. Evaluating computers: More sophisticated
EDP uses. *Nation's Cities*, 1975, *13*(10), 31-32.

Danziger, J. N. Service provider or skill bureaucracy?: The
data processing function from a data processing perspective. *Information*
Technology and Urban Governance. Ottawa, Canada: Ministry of State for
Urban Affairs, 1976, pp. 252-259.

Danziger, J. N. The importance of MIS-management: Data
processing from the management function perspective. *Papers presented for*
the Symposium on Information Technology and Urban Governance. Cana-
dian Government Conference Centre, Ottawa, Canada, February 24-26,
1976.

Danziger, J. N. Computers, local government, and the
litany to EDP. *Public Administration Review*, 1977, *37*(1), pp. 28-37.

Danziger, J. N., & Dutton, W. H. *Technological innovation*
in local government: The case of computers in U.S. cities and counties (Urban
Information Systems Research Project Working Paper, WP-76-12). Prepared for delivery at the Annual Meeting of the Midwest Political Science
Association, Chicago, Illinois, April 1976. Unpublished manuscript, University of California, Public Policy Research Organization, Irvine, CA, 1976.

Danziger, J. N., & Pearson, S. Executives vary in assessments. *County News*, 1975, *7*(40), pp. 10, 14.

Dutton, W. H. Major policy concerns facing local executives. *Nation's Cities*, 1975, *13*(10), 33-36.

Dutton, W. H., & King, J. L. Has the computer lived
up to billing? *County News*, 1975, *7*(40), pp. 11, 14.

Dutton, W. H., & Kraemer, K. L. Administrative reform,
technology, and intra-organizational power: Computers and management
control in local government. *Administration and Society* (forthcoming).

Dutton, W. H., & Kraemer, K. L. *Determinants of support
for computerized information systems* (Urban Information Systems Research
Project Working Paper WP-76-10). Unpublished manuscript, University of
California, Public Policy Research Organization, Irvine, CA, 1976.

Dutton, W. H., Kraemer, K. L., & Pearson, S. Chief
executives' view on information processing in local government. *Papers from
the 1975 Thirteenth Annual Conference on the Urban and Regional Information Systems Association*, 1976, Vol. I.

Dutton, W. H., & Pearson, S. Management information
top problem. *County News*, 1975, *7*(40), pp. 8, 10.

Dutton, W. H., & Pearson, S. Executives cite common
data system problems. *Nation's Cities*, 1975, *13*(10), 24-27.

Hackathorn, R. D. Data base management on minicomputers,
State Government Administration, June 1974.

Hackathorn, R. D. Technologies for information management. *Papers from the 1974 Twelfth Annual Conference of the Urban and
Regional Information Systems Association*, 1975, Vol. I.

King, J. L. Information control and privacy. *Papers from
the 1974 Twelfth Annual Conference of the Urban and Regional Information
Systems Association*, 1975, Vol. I.

King, J. L. Cost-benefit evaluation: A problematic
exercise in local government computing. *Papers from the 1975 Thirteenth
Annual Conference of the Urban and Regional Information Systems Association*, 1976, Vol. I.

Kling, R. The Riverville social services information
and referral system. *Papers from the 1975 Thirteenth Annual Conference of
the Urban and Regional Information Systems Association*, 1976, Vol. I.

Kraemer, K. L. Who really makes EDP decisions? *County
     News*, 1975, *7*(40), p. 12.

Kraemer, K. L. Who really is in charge of decisions
     about EDP? *Nation's Cities*, 1975, *13*(10), 37-40.

Kraemer, K. L. Local government, information systems,
     and technology transfer in the United States. *Information Technology and
     Urban Governance*. Ministry of State for Urban Affairs, Ottawa, Canada:
     1976, pp. 72-84.

Kraemer, K. L., Danziger, J. N., Dutton W. H., & Mood,
     A. M., with Kling, R. A future cities survey design for policy analysis.
     Socio-Economic Planning Sciences, 1976, *10*, 199-211.

Kraemer,, K. L., Danziger, J. N., & King, J. L. *Information
     technology and urban management in the United States* (Urban Information
     Systems Research Project Working Paper WP-76-14). Report prepared for
     The Panel on Information Technology and Urban Management of the Com-
     puter Utilization Group, Committee for Science Policy, Organization for
     Economic Cooperation and Development, Paris, France. Unpublished
     manuscript, University of California, Public Policy Research Organization,
     Irvine, CA, 1976.

Kraemer, K. L., Dutton, W. H., & Matthews, J. R. *Municipal
     computers: Growth, usage and management* (Urban Data Service Report
     11/75). Washington, D.C.: International City Management Association,
     1975, *7*(11).

Kraemer, K. L., & King, J. L. *Information systems, power,
     and executive control in local government* (Urban Information Systems Re-
     search Project Working Paper, WP-75-09). Unpublished manuscript, Uni-
     versity of California, Public Policy Research Organization, Irvine, CA,
     1975.

Kraemer, K. L., & King, J. L. The URBIS project: A
     policy-oriented study of computing in local government. *Papers from the
     1975 Thirteenth Annual Conference of the Urban and Regional Information
     Systems Association*, 1976, Vol. I.

Kraemer, K. L., Matthews, J. R., Dutton, W. H., &
     Hackathorn, L. D. *The municipal information systems directory*. Lexington,
     MA: Lexington, Books, 1976.

Kraemer, K. L., & Pearson, S. The computer finds a
     home in the county. *County News*, 1975, *7*(40), pp. 9, 14.

Kraemer, K. L., & Pearson, S. Chief executives say
they're sold on EDP. *Nation's Cities*, 1975, *13*(10), 20-23.

Matthews, J. R. Data access review boards and the management of installation security. *Papers from the 1974 Twelfth Annual Conference of the Urban and and Regional Information Systems Association*, 1975,
Vol. I.

Matthews, J. R. A survey of EDP performance measurement
for local government. *Papers from the 1975 Thirteenth Annual Conference
of the Urban and Regional Information Systems Association*, 1976. Vol. I.

Matthews, J. R., Dutton, W. H., & Kraemer, K. L. *County
computers: Growth, usage, and management* (Urban Data Service Report
2/76). Washington, D.C.: International City Management Association,
1976, *8*(2).

Matthews, J. R., & Kraemer, K. L. *Ten years of URISA
proceedings: Indexes and Abstracts*. Prepared for The Committee on URISA
Proceedings Index, Urban and Regional Information Systems Association.
Irvine, CA: University of California, Public Policy Research Organization,
1975.

Matthews, J. R., Kraemer, K. L., Hackathorn, L. D., &
Dutton, W. H. *The county information systems directory*. Lexington, MA:
Lexington Books, 1976.

Sartore, A. The people, technology, and organization
interface. *Papers from the 1974 Twelfth Annual Conference of the Urban and
Regional Information Systems Association*, 1975, Vol. I.

A MANAGER'S GLOSSARY OF COMPUTER-RELATED TERMS

This glossary is provided to assist the manager in understanding terminology common to computer-related activities. It is by no means exhaustive; rather it is an overview of the terms the manager is most likely to come in contact with. Also note that some of these terms have other definitions in addition to those shown here. These definitions refer only to computer-related use of these terms.

Also, at the end of this glossary, is a short guide to the full names of computer manufacturers that often are called by acronyms.

Access
Generally used as a noun meaning the ability to retrieve or place data in the computer, or to use the computer for data processing jobs. Sometimes used as a transitive verb, describing the act of gaining access: i.e., "to access a file."

Acronym
An acronym is a form of abbreviation, usually using the first letters of the words in a proper name. For example, NASA is an acronym for the National Aeronautics and Space Administration. Acronyms abound in the computing field.

ADP
See "Automatic Data Processing."

Alpha-numeric
A contraction of alphabetic-numeric, which refers to a set of symbols, often including the alphabet, numerals, and common punctuation.

Analyst
See "Systems Analyst."

Analog Computer
A computer that processes according to physical analogies, i.e., directly translates measures such as temperature, flow, voltage, or position into related electrical or mechanical quantities. Analog computers measure continuously. An analog computer can, for example, be used to continuously adjust traffic light signals to the flow of traffic measured by sensors in the street. Compare to "Digital Computer."

Application
A problem or need to which a computer is applied, such as a "payroll processing application."

Application Package
A routine or set or routines included in a computer program to perform the steps necessary for a particular application.

Automatic Data Processing
Data processing performed by a system of electronic or electromechanical machines, used to minimize the level of human effort and attention required.

Batch Processing
Refers to the practice of processing computer jobs in groups or "batches" that, once initiated, are entirely under control of the computer. Compare to "Interactive."

Baud
A unit of measure indicating the signal speed of data transmission, roughly equivalent to ten times the number of characters per second. (I.e., 300 baud = approximately 30 characters per second.)

BASIC
The name of a high-level computer language.

Bit
Actually an acronym for *bi*nary digi*t*. A binary digit is the basic symbolic element of binary code, the code on which digital computing is based. Often used as a measure of core or storage capacity.

Byte
A term used to describe a measure of consecutive bits. Depending on the kind of coding scheme in use, a byte will contain either 7 or 8 bits. A byte is roughly equivalent to a character in terms of size in storage.

Card
Sometimes called a Hollerith Card or IBM Card, refers to a card on which data can be keypunched for storage or inputting into the computer.

Card Reader
An input device that "reads" the keypunch holes in cards and translates these into input signals for the computer.

Cathode Ray Tube
Literally, a vacuum tube like a television picture tube that can be used as a display device for computer input or output. Often used as Cathode Ray Tube Terminal.

Central Processor
The main memory and processing section of the computer, containing the registers where computing actually takes place and the arithmetic computation circuits. The main controls for the computer are usually integrated to the central processor.

Character
Usually refers to one of a set of symbols such as the alphabet, the numerals 0-9, punctuation marks, etc. Sometimes used as a measure as in "5000 characters of storage." A character usually occupies a byte of storage space (see "Byte").

COBOL
An acronym for Common Business Oriented Language, a high-level computer language.

Compatibility
Usually refers to whether different pieces of computer equipment will match-up and operate with one another in a computer system.

Computer
Any device that accepts information, applies a predefined process to it, and outputs the results of the predefined process. Technically, a computer must be able to (1) accept information (INPUT), (2) store information (MEMORY), (3) receive instruction (PROGRAMS) on how to deal with information, and (4) play out the results of the jobs it is instructed to perform (OUTPUT).

Core Or Core Memory
Refers to Magnetic Core Storage, but often is synonomous with the main memory storage of the computer, since most computers use magnetic core storage as their main working storage.

Data
Plural of "datum," which is a representation of a fact in a formalized manner that is capable of being manipulated or communicated by a process. Data are the building blocks of "information."

Data Base (Databank)
Refers to a collection of data of similar kind, accumulated over time and kept to serve multiple needs for data. A data base is essentially synonomous with databank, though a databank is sometimes thought of as a collection of large data bases.

Data Base Management
A concept for manipulating data by creating programs that "move through" a data base, selecting specific data items and performing operations using them.

Data Base Management System
An interrelated set of computer programs that enables use of the data base management concept.

DBMS
See "Data Base Management System."

Dedication
Refers to confinement of a computer or computer installation to performing data processing for a particular purpose, task, or agency.

Digital Computer
A computer that processes information represented discretely or discontinuously. It can perform arithmetic or logical operations on both data and its own programs. It stores programs internally. Compare "Analog Computer."

Disc Storage (Disk)
Refers to a mode of storage in which information is coded onto the magnetic surface of a rotating disc.

Diskette
See "Floppy-Disk."

Drive
A device used to operate a mass storage medium such as a disc, magnetic tape, drum, or floppy-disk:

Drum Storage
Refers to a mode of computer storage in which information is coded onto the magnetic surface of a rotating drum or cylinder. Drum storage is typically faster for storage and retrieval than disc or tape storage.

EAM
See "Electrical Accounting Machine."

EDP
See "Electronic Data Processing."

Electrical Accounting Machine
Mechanical devices that perform accounting by using punch cards; tabulating, sorting, and storing capabilities are common features.

Electronic Data Processing
Data processing performed using electronic equipment, usually modern electronic computers. Often distinguishes strictly computerized data processing from data processing using other automatic machinery (See "ADP").

Emulation
A process using computer hardware that allows a computer program written for one kind of computer to be run on a different kind of computer.

File
Any organized collection of information directed toward some purpose, and usually complete for that purpose, e.g., an address file.

Floppy-Disk Or Diskette
A relatively new storage medium using a flexible, magnetically coated disc that remains stationary and is easily removed from its drive unit.

FORTRAN
An acronym for *For*mula *Tran*slation Language, a high-level computer language frequently used in scientific and engineering applications of computers.

Geographic Base File
A file of data organized according to geographic identifiers (e.g., street address or land parcels) that serves as a data base for planning, analysis, and operations purposes.

Geoprocessing
A contraction of Geographic Processing, referring to any data processing activity that makes use of data organized by geographic identifiers.

Graphics Terminal
A computer terminal containing a television-like screen capable of displaying computer output in graphic form, such as figures, pictures, line drawings, etc.

Hard Copy
Refers to documents containing data printed by data processing equipment, which can be permanently stored. Usually refers to printed paper.

Hardware
Refers to the actual equipment of the computer system, such as the main-frame and peripherals. Compare to "Software."

High-Level Language
A language used for instructing the computer, but which is addressed to solving the problem the computer is working on rather than on instructing the operations of the computer machinery. Must be used in conjunction with operating software. Examples of such languages: BASIC, FORTRAN, CO-BOL.

Housekeeping
Commonly refers to those activities in computer operations that do not contribute to execution of user programs, but rather "keep the system going." Also used in the sense of "Housekeeping Application" to refer to any routine, relatively simple computer application used for day to day operational assistance in an organization (e.g., payroll accounting).

Input
The process of transferring data from a store (e.g., punch cards, lists, magnetic tapes) into the computer, using an input device such as a card reader, terminal, or tape drive.

Interactive
Refers to Interactive Computing, in which the user is able to carry on a "dialogue" with the computer using a terminal. Compare to "Batch Processing."

Interface
Any shared boundary; in computing usually indicates boundary between pieces of equipment connected to one another.

I/O
An abbreviation for Input/Output. Refers to the equipment and/or process for controlling inputs from users to the computer and outputs from the computer back to users.

Keypunch
A machine with a typewriter keyboard and other special symbols that can punch small holes in data cards to record data on them.

Line Printer
A device capable of printing a complete line of type across a page with a single strike. Some line printers can print up to 1600 lines per minute.

Machine Language
A very basic computer language consisting only of instructions that can be directly understood by the computing machine.

Machine-Readable Form
Refers to data stored in such a way that they can be "read" or directly inputted into the computer through a machine-controlled input device such as a tape drive or card reader.

Magnetic Core Storage
See "Core Storage."

Magnetic Tape
A tape with a magnetic surface on which data can be stored by polarization (just like in a tape recorder).

Mapping
The process of transforming information from one form into another.

Main Frame
Refers to that part of the computer containing the control processor and basic operating controls.

Memory
A device in a computer for storage of information. Several different kinds of memory exist. See "Core Memory"; "Virtual Memory."

Multi-Processing
Simultaneous processing of two or more programs in a single computer system. Not same as Multi-Programming.

Multi-Programming
A technique for handling numerous programs at the same time by overlapping or interweaving their execution. Most common attribute of Time-shared computer systems. Not same as multi-processing, which actually executes two or more programs simultaneously without interweaving or overlapping.

Network
Refers in computing to the linking-together of two or more computers so messages can be exchanged and in some cases so processing can be shared.

Off-Line
A computer-related activity performed apart from the computer, usually on another piece of hardware, that may be run on the computer. Not under control of the central processor.

On-Line
Refers to being under control of the central processing unit, usually in the case of a device capable of receiving input or providing output on a real-time basis. Commonly applied as "on-line terminals."

Operating System
Any of several kinds of programs that control the actual operational activities of the computer. Usually specific to particular machines, and usually provided by the computer manufacturer for its machines.

Operator
Or Computer Operator; the person who operates the computer's controls, mounts and unmounts magnetic tapes from tape drives, puts new paper in the line printer, and so on.

Output
The process of transferring data from an internal store on the computer (such as core memory or on-line disc storage) to some external store or display (such as a line printer or terminal).

Paper Tape
A tape made of paper that can be punched with holes to record data in a manner similar to data cards, and can be read by a paper-tape reader attached to the computer. A form of machine-readable, hard copy storage.

Peripheral Equipment
All of the input, output, and auxilliary (non-core or virtual) storage devices of a computer. I.e., any hardware in the computer system not a part of the central processor.

Programmer
A programmer is an individual who translates the concept of a computer application, as devised by a systems analyst, into a computer program that instructs the computer to carry out the operations necessary for the application.

Real-Time
Refers in computing parlance to the operation of a computing system in a sufficiently fast manner to allow the results of computation to influence the process being monitored or controlled. A "real-time system" often designates a system that is capable of operating interactively with a user.

Remote Job Entry
Refers to the process of entering or inputting and receiving output from an input-output device located some distance away from the computer, but attached to it through communication cables.

RJE
See "Remote Job Entry."

Report Program Generator
A special kind of computer program that generates other programs to control routine report-writing functions of the computer. For example, will automatically write a program to format an output report based on input data with no original format.

RPG
An acronym for *R*eport *P*rogram *G*enerator; also the trade name of a program that is a report program generator.

Response Time
The time-lag between an input and the corresponding output.

Security
In the case of computers, two kinds of security are at issue: installation security, referring to the security of the computer installation itself; and system security, referring to the security of the data and programs in the computer or its storage devices.

Software
The programs and routines used to facilitate the use of a computer. Compare with "Hardware."

Source Document
A document from which data is taken, such as a coding sheet used by a keypunch operator.

Storage
See "Memory." Note: sometimes preferred over memory as a term for describing a device in which data can be accumulated and stored.

Systems Analyst
A systems analyst is an individual who analyzes a need for a computer application and designs the application in light of the user's needs and the computer system's capabilities. Usually, the systems analyst gives his finished design to a programmer who writes the application program.

Tape Drive
See "Drive."

Teleprocessing
Refers to use of a computer facility remote from the user, generally through a terminal transmitting and receiving data over telephone or data lines.

Terminal
Technically, refers to any point in a computer system at which data can enter or leave the system. Commonly refers to an input-output device using a keyboard and some kind of display, such as a hard copy printer (teletypewriter) or cathode ray tube display.

Time-Sharing
Refers to the use of the computer for two or more purposes during the same general time interval, usually accomplished by "swapping" and scheduling different user's jobs among the various components of the computer (e.g., core memory, disc storage, line printer, etc.), thus allowing most of the components to be operating on at least part of someone's job all the time. Time-sharing is often a key element in multi-programming computing situations.

Updating
Incorporation into a master file of changes reflecting recent transactions or other events performed by the computer.

Virtual Memory
Or Virtual Storage. Refers to a technique for increasing the effective core memory (core storage) of a computer by dividing large processing tasks into sequences, and temporarily storing those sequences preceding and following

the processing being done at the moment on a high-speed on-line storage device such as a drum or special disc storage unit. As the name implies, virtual memory provides the computer with extra memory that is "virtually" equivalent to core memory. Usually less expensive than adding actual core memory.

Word
Any group of bits or characters treated as a unit and capable of being stored in a single storage cell in the computer memory. Often used as a measure in computers, particularly when describing the main processing capability of a computer. Larger computers tend to have registers with larger word-lengths, expressed in bits. For example, an IBM System 3 has 8 bit word-length, while the much larger IBM System 370 has a 32 bit word-length.

A Short Guide to Computer Manufacturer
Names Commonly Expressed in Acronyms

Acronym
Full Company Name

CDC
Control Data Corporation

DEC
Digital Equipment Corporation

HP
Hewlett-Packard

HIS
Honeywell Information Systems

IBM
International Business Machines

NCR
National Cash Register

ABOUT THE AUTHORS

KENNETH L. KRAEMER is Director of the Public Policy Research Organization and Associate Professor of Administration at the University of California, Irvine. He currently is principal investigator on the URBIS Project, a nation-wide study of information systems in local governments. He has contributed articles on government information systems to both scholarly and professional journals, including *The International Review of Administrative Sciences*, *Public Administration Review* and *Nation's Cities*, and is an author and co-author of several books and monographs, among them *Computers, Power, and Urban Management*, *Policy Analysis in Local Government*, *Integrated Municipal Information Systems*, *The Municipal Information Systems Directory*, and *The County Information Systems Directory*. Professor Kraemer has served as a consultant to numerous government programs dealing with electronic data processing, including the USAC Integrated Municipal Information Systems projects, and has participated in international programs such as the Panel on Information Technology and Urban Management of the Organization for Economic Cooperation and Development (OECD), and the Joint Soviet-American Program on Application of Computers to Management of Large Cities. He holds a Ph.D. in Public Administration from the University of Southern California.

JOHN LESLIE KING is a research specialist with the Public Policy Research Organization of the University of California, Irvine. He has been involved in research into government information systems since 1972, and is currently a member of the URBIS Project research staff. He is author of several research monographs and professional articles on subjects related to government use of electronic data processing, including privacy and confidentiality, cost-benefit analysis, and information systems development, and is co-author of *Computers, Power, and Urban Management*. He has been a consultant to numerous programs providing guidance to cities and counties in use of data processing, and is a member of the Committee on Computers and Public Policy of the Association for Computing Machinery (ACM). Mr. King holds a M.S. degree in Administration and is currently a Ph.D. candidate in Administration at the University of California, Irvine.

THE COMPUTER AND AFRICA: Applications, Problems, and Potential
   edited by
   D.R.F. Taylor
   R.A. Obudho

*COST-BENEFIT ANALYSIS: New and Expanded Edition
   E.J. Mishan

POLICY EVALUATION FOR COMMUNITY DEVELOPMENT:
Decision Tools for Local Government
   Shimon Awerbuch
   William A. Wallace

*Also available in paperback as a PSS Student Edition.